Social Working

Edited by

Pam Carter, Tony Jeffs and Mark K. Smith

Consultant Editor: Jo Campling

MACMILLAN

First published 1995 by
THE MACMILLAN PRESS LTD
Houndmills, Basingstoke, Hampshire RG21 2XS
and London
Companies and representatives
throughout the world

ISBN 0–333–60910–7 hardcover
ISBN 0–333–60911–5 paperback

A catalogue record for this book is available
from the British Library.

Printed in Hong Kong

Contents

Preface

Social Working is an attempt to provide a framework for thinking about the daily (and not so daily) experiences of being a social worker. Our concern was to foster an environment in which a number of workers could write about their practice including what they actually do, feel and think. Many of the central experiences and processes of social work have either been ignored by writers or have been approached in some grand schematic way. We wanted to encourage people to look again at what being a social worker involves. This is particularly important currently when social workers are having to defend the importance of social work values and processes in a very hostile climate.

Social work practice is frequently categorized in terms of client groups, methods or settings. This book focuses instead on processes which to a considerable extent cut across these different categories. Attention to these often taken for granted processes leads us to examine the links between experiencing, thinking and doing which lie at the heart of practice. We selected what appeared to us to be some of the main processes which practitioners undertake:

for themselves
- organizing the daily round
- keeping records and recording

with clients
- policing
- counselling
- educating
- advising and advocating
- living alongside

and with colleagues
- supervising
- managing staff
- teamworking

Each of these processes is the focus for a chapter. All these chapters are written by workers. A short introduction to each piece is provided by us as editors. These are intended to identify some of the ways in which readers might use the accounts to facilitate their own reflectiveness. We have also added two chapters. The first asks some basic questions about practice, and how we relate feelings, thoughts and actions to each other; the second draws together a number of the threads that run through the book and places the material in its broader political and organizational contexts.

At the end of each chapter we have added a number of questions. Mostly these were suggested by the workers. We did this because we thought that these, like our introductory comments, may help individual readers to take some of the issues further. We also hope chapters might be used to provide a focus for team sessions and seminars.

The picture of practice that emerges is far from perfect. You are not about to read a series of glowing accounts. Instead, you will find a group of workers struggling to make sense of their experiences and what they see other social workers doing. A picture of the daily realities of social working emerges. However, something more also appears: these workers are not simply describing what they do and see, and they are not merely applying theories learnt in colleges or read in books. They are active theory-makers themselves, but, because these are theories-in-practice, they are not always tidy and do not attempt to be universal. More than anything else, we hope that this book will encourage readers to engage as theory-makers in the less than perfect world of their own work.

PAM CARTER
TONY JEFFS
MARK K. SMITH

Notes on the Contributors

Irene Boyd is working as a team manager in a child care team in Newcastle social services. She has a range of experience with children and families in pre-school education and community work.

Pam Carter is a lecturer in the Department of Economics and Government and the Social Welfare Research Unit, University of Northumbria at Newcastle.

Val Chapman is team leader of a child protection team. Her background is in community social work.

Tony Jeffs is a lecturer in the Department of Applied Social Science, the University of Northumbria at Newcastle.

Jennifer Lapompe is a social work manager working with young people experiencing difficulties. She has experience in youth social work and youth and community work.

Patsy Little was, at the time of writing, a deputy project leader in a youth justice centre. She is currently a community education officer.

Deborah Mann has several years' experience of community and youth work. She is currently working as a warden in a homeless families hostel.

Deborah Marshall has eleven years' experience in probation. She is currently a senior probation officer. Her previous probation work has included specialisms in community service and domestic work.

Celia Parnell is Gateshead Social Services Department Child Protection Co-ordinator. She has worked as a social worker in a number of local authorities.

Jane Skittrall works in Newcastle as a child-care social worker. She has experience in youth work and groupwork.

Mark K. Smith is Tutor and Research Fellow, Centre for Professional Studies in Informal Education, YMCA National College, London.

Lynnzie Stirling is currently a mental health social worker in an area team. She has experience of residential work and of generic field social work.

Mary Turner is the director of a voluntary counselling and training agency in Merseyside. She is involved in supervisor training and supervises staff, volunteers and students.

Jeremy Walker has worked for Wandsworth social services for 15 years, the last 7 specializing in mental health. He has recently completed psychotherapy training.

The views expressed are those of the contributors and should in no way be taken to represent those of their employers or other agencies with which they are connected.

1

Introduction: Thinking about Practice in Social Work

PAM CARTER, TONY JEFFS and MARK K. SMITH

I have five colleagues in the district and apart from one they haven't got a clue about talking about their own work practice. There are all sorts of interesting things going on there. I can see people thinking 'Oh I don't really want to talk about that, what will people think?' Until they do they are missing so much.

It's when you link a theory or idea with real life things and you have one of those moments where you have a flash 'that is what that is'. This can happen while you are working with a client. However, it is often afterwards in reflection or analysis that things become clear – thinking about it yourself and talking it over in supervision.

Looking at what we do as workers can be taxing and threatening. We have to take a step back, get in touch with our feelings, thoughts and actions, and try to make sense of experiences. These are not easy things to do and what we find is not always welcome. In the same way, sharing work with others can often seem like a risky business. On the one hand we may learn and develop from the experience; on the other, we may look fools or failures.

Our questions, doubts and pleasures with regard to our practice thus can easily remain hidden or be put to one side. In the chapters that follow, a number of workers take the plunge. They describe, and reflect on, key aspects of their work. However, before we look at these, we too need to take a step back and ask a couple of preliminary questions. First, what is it about those workers we recognize as good or special, the real artists, that sets them apart? Second, what actually do we mean when we talk of 'practice'?

Professional artistry and social working

Social work involves more than gaining and exercising technical knowledge and skills: it depends on us also cultivating a kind of artistry. In this sense, 'professional' workers are not technicians applying their skills to carry out a plan or drawing: they are artists who are able to improvise and devise new ways of looking at things. This comes out in the quotations we used to begin this chapter. The second worker felt able to react to situations as they arose because she had an understanding of some of the different things that were likely to happen. However, each situation is different. As Cynthia Parnell says in a later chapter, there is little that is routine or predictable in social work. As a result, central to what we do as workers is the ability to 'think on our feet'.

Yet while each situation may be unique, we still need to 'maintain a settled practice, a set of routines and patterns of action' (Louden, 1991, p. xi). There are limits to what we can handle. This comes out in many of the accounts that follow. We develop patterns of working, and resolutions to familiar social work problems. These are shaped by our biography and professional experience. For example, in Chapter 5, Deborah Marshall describes how she moved from organizing her practice around a welfaring model and faced up to policing. We can see the interplay of experience and reflection in her account. The familiar patterns of working or routines that she develops also allow her to improvise. Like dancers who have learnt their basic steps, we can combine and recombine moves into new patterns. We literally 'think on our feet' or reflect-in-action (Schön, 1983). When things go wrong, or we are faced with something unknown, then we can always fall back on tried and tested ways of doing things or 'procedures' to carry us through.

Describing social work as an art does sound a bit pretentious. It may also appear twee, but there is a serious point here. When we listen to other workers – for example, in team meetings – or have the chance to observe them in action, we inevitably form judgments about their ability. At one level, for example, we might be impressed by someone's knowledge of the benefit system or of the effects of different drugs.

However, such knowledge is useless if it cannot be used in the best way. We may be informed and be able to draw on a range of techniques, yet the thing that makes us special is the way in which we are able to combine these and improvise regarding the particular situation. It is this quality that we are describing as artistry.

For Schön (1987, p. 13) artistry is an exercise of intelligence, a kind of knowing. It is a quality that can be seen in what Jeremy Walker, for example, says about his work in an area office (Chapter 4). Through sustained study of experience he is able to draw out a series of maxims about counselling. We see many examples of this quality in the chapters that follow. It can be found in our ability to reflect-in-, and on-action, and as part of that we have to foster, in Eisner's words, 'connoisseurship and ... criticism' (1985, pp. 87–102).

What is practice?

Before we look in more detail at professional reflection we must return to the question, 'What is practice?' This might seem a bit odd. It is obvious, some would say; practice is what we *do* as workers. A number of books about social work education seem to share this view. 'Practice' is left undefined or is not seen as a problem (e.g., Butler and Elliot, 1985; Danbury, 1986). But what constitutes 'practice' is not that obvious.

A common way of starting to answer this question is to put something called 'theory' on one side, and this thing called 'practice' on the other. In this approach theories are sets of abstract ideas and hypotheses developed, for example, by academics. Practitioners are then expected to 'apply' these to situations and problems. We might take ideas developed by social psychologists concerning the way groups form (e.g., Turner, 1987) and employ them to explain events in a group. This is an approach often taken by those setting student essays. Underpinning this is a tendency to see the social sciences as *the* foundation for practice. It is a viewpoint which:

> assumes that professional knowledge is based on theory from which is derived general principles (or rules) which can be applied to the 'instrumental problems' of practice. Theory is therefore privileged as 'real' knowledge whilst practice, seen as consisting merely of skills, is taken to be the *application* of that knowledge to the solving of problems. (Usher and Bryant, 1989, p. 71)

One problem that many of us face is that the theories we find in textbooks do not fit the situation we are exploring. We have to bend 'facts' to fit the theory, or we simply give up because the theory is so vague. As Coulshed (1988) suggests, many of the theories we borrow from the social and behavioural sciences are inconsistent and speculative. As a result of this, she argues, 'the application of theory to practice has to be tentative and uncertain' (p. 5).

We question this way of seeing theory and practice as separate from one another. If practice is the act of doing something then it cannot be considered in isolation from what a person is thinking. All actions have some aim or intention. At any one time we may not be conscious of these, but they are there, often heavily overlaid by feelings. For an intention to be linked to an action there has to be theory. An example here might help. Workers will sometimes talk to parents about the importance of play to their children. They may even work with the parents so that they can learn to play with their children. To do this workers must have some theory: perhaps that play helps the bonding process, or that it fosters learning. However, this theory may be buried very deep or may simply be implicit in the ways of working we have built for ourselves.

Practice, we suggested earlier, involves a set of routines and patterns of action. These patterns 'cannot be observed in the same way as natural objects. They can only be interpreted by reference to the actor's motives, intentions or purposes in performing the action' (Carr and Kemmis, 1986, p. 88). This is crucial. It means we have to move beyond believing that practice is in some simple way dependent on theory: rather, the two are linked. We cannot talk of practice without talking of theory (Usher and Bryant, 1989, p. 79). '"Practice" cannot be lacking theory. Similarly, it is difficult to conceive of "theory" that is "purely" descriptive and devoid of reference to purposeful action. The attempt to understand in social work has an action goal (or is practice) in itself' (Pilalis, 1986, p. 92). In other words Pilalis argues that practice is soaked in theory. It is theory in action.

Yet there is more at work here. Practice does not only involve thinking and acting: it is also tied to our values, our ideas about what makes for good. Judgments about what we are doing link intimately with feelings and values. This comes across strongly in Deborah Mann's exploration of living and working in a homeless family unit (Chapter 6). Her accounts of work with different individuals bring out just how much our judgments are wrapped up with our values. She also highlights the critical importance of staying in touch with our feelings. Our actions hold within them some view of the world. We may not be aware of this for much of the time, but we cannot escape it. Thus, our interest as workers should not only be with informed action; it needs also to be with committed action.

Our actions as social workers should express certain commitments. We should be seeking to foster feelings, thoughts and actions that enhance human well-being and social justice. In each situation we have to make a judgment. To do this we must have a certain disposition. As Buchman comments, people cannot practise, 'take part and share, in association with others – when they are mean spirited and dishonest' (1990, p. 48), as well as ignorant or careless about the extent to which human well-being is enhanced.

What we are arguing here is that within social work we must develop an understanding of practice as *praxis*: as informed, committed action. That is to say, practice is the interaction of theory-making, judgment and action. We must attend to the way in which we think, feel and act; and what informs such processes. The problem facing many of us is that it sometimes feels like there is not the space for these sorts of choices. We are told to do things; or we have to follow certain guidelines.

Theory

From what we have been saying it should be clear that we believe that workers and students are just as much theory-makers as academics who write books. This is not to say that they always use the same approach or focus on the same things. However, both must sort out and connect the things they encounter. Each has to identify the general properties which explain the events observed.

One way of distinguishing between the two has been to suggest that academics are primarily concerned with 'grand theory' and 'middle range theory'. Grand theory provides a comprehensive conceptual scheme; middle-range theory focuses on specific aspects of society (e.g., labelling theory) or ways of approaching practice (e.g., task-centred casework: see Payne, 1991, p. 56). In contrast, workers can be seen as trying to develop 'situational theories'. Their interest is in enhancing their thinking about a situation. To work with a client they need an idea of the possible consequences of the actions they may take.

The problem with this distinction is that it can quickly become overblown. Workers need 'grand theory'; academics must attend to the particular. As Geertz puts it, there has to be a continuous tacking back and forth:

> between the most local of local detail and the most global of global structure in such a way as to bring both into view simultaneously ... Hopping back and forth between the whole conceived through the parts which actualize it and the parts conceived through the whole which motivates them, we seek to turn them, by a sort of intellectual perpetual motion, into explications of one another. (Geertz, 1983, p. 69)

Another way of looking at the theory-making of academics and workers is to make a distinction between formal and informal theory. Again this is something we are not happy with. Formal theories can be seen as organized, codified bodies of knowledge, which are most commonly embodied in disciplines or subjects such as psychology and sociology (Usher, 1989, p. 80). They use 'academic' conventions, such as references to various books and articles, and 'academic' forms of expression. In contrast, informal theories are the ideas or frameworks used by workers, often unconsciously, to make sense of daily situations.

There are dangers in pushing this too far. Formal theory is not the sole possession of academics. Workers also build formal theories. Some, like the contributors to this book, may commit their ideas to paper for others to read; many others do not. However, in supervision or in reading case notes they organize their thinking into recognizable forms. There may also be a similar concern with rigour. This is surely one of the messages that Patsy Little tries to give in her piece on records and record keeping (Chapter 3). The care with which she approaches recording, and the use she makes of it in developing ideas and theories about her work, are also echoed in academic disciplines such as anthropology (see, e.g., Sanjek, 1990). Perhaps, then, the most useful way of thinking about academic and worker theories lies in differences in the use of language and conventions, and in presentation.

However, one distinction we do need to hold on to is that between theories which are implicit in what we do as workers and academics, and those on which we call to speak of our actions to others. The former can be described as 'theories-in-use'. They govern actual behaviour and tend to be tacit structures. Their relation to action 'is like the relation of grammar-in-use to speech; they contain assumptions about self, others and environment – these assumptions constitute a microcosm of science in everyday life' (Argyris and Schön, 1974, p. 30). The words we use to convey what we do, or what we would like others to think we do, can then be called 'espoused theory'.

Making this distinction allows us to ask questions about the extent to which behaviour fits espoused theory; and whether inner feelings become expressed in actions. In other words, is there congruence between the two? For example, in explaining our actions to a tutor or supervisor we may call upon some convenient piece of theory. We might explain our sudden rush out of the office to others, or even to ourselves at some level, by saying that a 'crisis' has arisen in one of 'our' families. The theory-in-use might be quite different. We may have become bored and tired by the paperwork or meeting and felt that a quick trip out to an apparently difficult situation would bring welcome relief. Much of the business of supervision, where it is focused on the practitioner's thoughts, feelings and actions (see Chapter 9), is concerned with the gulf between espoused theory and theory-in-use or in bringing the latter to the surface. This gulf is no bad thing. If it gets too wide then there is clearly a difficulty but, provided the two remain connected, then the gap creates a dynamic for reflection and for dialogue.

Reflecting-in and on-action

When we say that certain people are able to reflect-in-action what is it that they are able to do? In many respects reflecting-in-action can be likened to thinking on our feet, as we saw earlier. As we work with an individual or group we listen to what is said and observe what is going on. At the same time we try to make sense of the experience. This then helps us to make decisions about how to act (or not act). Schön describes the process thus:

> The practitioner allows himself to experience surprise, puzzlement, or confusion in a situation which he finds uncertain or unique. He reflects on the phenomenon before him, and on the prior understandings which have been implicit in his behaviour. He carries out an experiment which serves to generate both a new understanding of the phenomenon and a change in the situation. (Schön, 1983, p. 68)

The process boils down to the following. We reflect on what has happened or is happening; we develop ideas, explanations, hypotheses;

and we act based on this new understanding. There are four main elements. We:

(a) engage with or in the situation;
(b) go back over our experiences and feelings;
(c) evaluate any connections with previous understandings and thoughts; and
(d) develop a new and tentative understanding that allows us to frame and test our response (see Smith, forthcoming).

We then re-engage, and so on. This is happening all the time. It is not a process that we follow mechanically: instead, there are all sorts of jumps and hesitations. No set rules are laid down (Dewey, 1933, p. 207).

In this we move beyond established ideas and techniques, such as the pure knowledge of the textbook and so on. Rather, we develop an understanding of each case we encounter. We have to think things through, for every case is unique. When we forget this, problems arise. If we simply label people as a 'housing problem' or whatever, and then go through our 'housing routine', we are liable to miss all sorts of things. We are not really listening to the other person as a person, but rather as an object. Of course, we rely on routines: it would be intolerable if we had to work things out from first principles for each and every situation. However, those routines have to be open to feedback from the situation. We think 'on the hoof'. This means that we do not have to have a full understanding before we act: this way of working involves us in forming hypotheses or leading ideas which we can test in action. Workers begin with an idea of what makes for the good and then work out what that means to the situations in which they find themselves.

In this there is an important distinction between reflecting-in-action and reflection-on-action. Reflecting-in-action involves thinking things through as we work. We reflect in time to act, we reflect in the present. Reflection-on-action is something we do after the event. We may do this, as Patsy Little suggests, through writing up our recordings (see Chapter 3). We may also talk things through with a supervisor (see Chapter 9), share matters with team members (see Chapter 2) or just sit down and mull over matters by ourselves. As Mary Turner puts it, through thinking better, we can deal more effectively with the confusion and anxiety inherent in our work (Chapter 9).

To exercise our artistry we need to both reflect-on- and in-action. The act of reflecting-on-action enables us to spend time exploring why we worked in a particular way, what was happening in the group, and so on. This is time that we do not have when we are in the thick of things. As we look at experiences, we develop a set of questions and ideas about practice. These we take into future situations. As we work we can then use these questions and ideas. They form a repertoire from which we draw to enable us to think about what is happening as it is happening. When ordered into routines and patterns, ideas and associated actions can help us to handle difficult situations.

We have to think in a particular way as we act, and that thinking is deeply influenced by what has gone before. It is also conditioned by the repertoire of ideas and images we bring, and our disposition and values as practitioners. Our values will be significantly shaped by our own identities and subjectivities: our place in the social world. Racism, sexism, heterosexism and other forms of oppression, as well as resistance to them, will have an important influence on what we bring to our work. As we work we can bring fragments of ideas and theories, and pieces of previous experiences and situations into play. We begin to build responses that fit the new situation. In this we are not the passive appliers of preformed theories or practice wisdom: we are theory-makers. We draw on various scraps, patterns, routines, yet this is not a glorified form of eclecticism. While we may gather our images and ideas from all over, they have be woven into a pattern. They are shaped by our intelligence and our commitment to certain values and beliefs. This is what Lynnzie Stirling means when she talks about advocacy as being a state of mind, a constant sensitivity to opportunities for helping clients to act on their own behalf (Chapter 7).

At the same time we have to handle the fact that there is much that we do not, and cannot, know about the situation or experience. We have to live and work with uncertainties and half-formed ideas. In these circumstances we can take small, cautious steps or large, imaginative leaps. Whatever, we need to avoid jumping to closed conclusions and keep open the possibility of change as a result of reflecting-in-action and dialogue with others. The goals we have may not always be clear but, as Jane Skittrall and Irene Boyd put it, we try to work in a deliberate way (Chapter 8). So what is involved in this act of reflection?

Boud, Keogh and Walker argue that in reflection people 'recapture their experience, think about it, mull it over and evaluate it' (1985, p. 19). We return to and explore our experiences to enhance our understandings and appreciations. Three elements are important in the process:

(a) *returning to experience*: that is to say, recollecting or describing salient events;
(b) *attending to (or connecting with) feelings*: this has two aspects, utilizing helpful feelings and removing or containing obstructive ones;
(c) *evaluating experience*: this involves re-examining experience in the light of one's intent and existing knowledge, etc. It also involves integrating this new knowledge into the person's conceptual framework (see Boud, Keogh and Walker, 1985, pp. 26–31).

To examine material we have to assemble it. In action we may quickly replay what has just happened and attempt to retrieve salient details. Through further conversation we may build a fuller picture. We may sit down and write up the experience in recordings. In these we attempt to recount what occurred, what were our actions and feelings, and what were those of others. We try to identify the various elements in the situation. We may even take the experience to supervision or talk it through with a colleague or friend. By re-observing the experience we hope to see further details and patterns. In a sense we also seek to externalize the material, to step outside it so that we may approach it from another angle. This then enables us to act.

Looking at the social work process and frame of reference

While much is written about the differences between social work traditions (e.g., between behavioural and task-centred work), we tend to agree with Payne (1991) that the shared elements are of great significance. He lists some common features in the social context of social work and their implications:

(a) people are treated as *individuals*, not categories;
(b) clients and actions are understood through *psychological and social knowledge*, evidence and argument;
(c) social work operates through *relationships*;
(d) social work uses the *organizational context* of its relationships to carry out its activities;
(e) social work defines *need*;
(f) social work is concerned with *maintaining important social structures*;
(g) social work *advocates* for clients (see Payne, 1991, p. 23).

We may question some of these, but this listing has the virtue of high-lighting some key ideas, ideals and relationships that help shape the social work frame of reference. They help to define how people come to understand themselves as social workers and what their role might be. Also contained within them are hints of the 'exalted ideals that beckon a social worker' (Biestek, 1961, p. 136): principles such as client self-determination, confidentiality and individualization. In other words, workers must have both a personal idea of what makes for human well-being, and one which is shared by others.

When we place such ideas besides those of Schön and the other writers discussed here we begin to see the shape of the social work process. Social work is a practical activity which requires practical reasoning. Being 'practical' is not something second rate: rather, it involves grounding our theory-making in judgments about what makes for well-being, and what is happening in relationships and events. It is a sophisticated form of thinking. Workers have to allow themselves to experience surprise and puzzlement: to make the familiar strange. They think about the phenomena they are seeing or experiencing, while drawing on previous understandings, so that they become researchers in the practice context:

When someone reflects-in-action ... he is not dependent on the categories of established theory and technique, but constructs a new theory of the unique case. His inquiry is not limited to deliberation about means which depend on a prior agreement about ends. He does not keep means and ends separate, but defines them interactively as he frames a problematic situation. He does not separate thinking from doing, ratiocinating his way to a decision which he must later convert to action. Because his experimenting is a kind of action, implementation is built into his inquiry. (Schön, 1983, p. 68)

When we consider this in the context of social work intervention, then we have to revise common, linear, ways of thinking. For example, the Pincus and Minahan (1973) model has certain stages or practice skill areas (we could have chosen several other models here, such as that of Davies, 1985). Their model of the social work process is as follows:

Assessing the problem
Collecting data
Making initial contacts
Negotiating contracts

Forming action systems
Maintaining and co-ordinating action systems
Exercising influence
Terminating the change effort

It is a pattern repeated in the more influential neighbourhood work texts (e.g., Henderson and Thomas, 1987). Most such models draw upon industrial or bureaucratic forms of thinking and practice. More specifically they focus on objectives and outcomes (products). Such approaches tend to stress technical rationality. The problem is described, then analysed, and a desired outcome and objectives framed. The method is then chosen, evaluation criteria and mechanisms established and steps taken to implement the project. All this then feeds back into the understanding of the problem.

We chose the Pincus and Minihan model because of its close affinity to the language of community care. As Cochrane (1993, p. 80) has argued, implementation of the 1990 National Health Service and Community Care Act has involved a 'clear and unequivocal move' away from casework approaches.

Instead social workers – possibly renamed care managers – are intended to act as co-ordinators putting together packages of care for individuals on the basis of assessments of need and identifying others ... to meet these needs.

As the balance moves towards management we are left with basic questions about what this work is – it certainly need not be done by a social worker (Audit Commission, 1992). At the same time there have been moves to deskill direct caring functions, 'by devolving them to poorly trained (and poorly paid) care workers or to the voluntary or informal sectors' (Langan, 1993, p. 164). These aspects are not only changing – they appear to be moving beyond the boundaries of a narrowing definition of the social work task.

Social work has also been hit by legislation, codes of practice and various guidelines in both the child protection and mental health arenas. One impact of these has been to constrain the activities of workers for fear of their facing both managerial and legal challenges. With this has come a change in language – less is said about growth or treatment, and rather more about protection and 'managing risk'. Yet, there are countervailing forces. The increased emphasis on interdisciplinary and multi-agency working, and the need to develop specialisms demands more sophisticated practice. Traditional casework, as described by Payne (1991), will still be required – although the context in which it takes place may well alter. Other ways of working – such as those discussed in this book – will also be needed, and these all entail moving beyond crude, technical models of practice.

We therefore want to argue for another way of approaching practice– one that stresses reflection and deliberation. Rather than starting with the problem, a reflective approach allows a number of elements to interact at any one moment. The talk is not so much of objectives, but of how our ideas of what makes for human flourishing interact with particular situations, and how critical thinking may be generated and applied. We might call this a practice or process approach to social work, and it has a number of important implications for the way in which we work. In particular, it means that we have to look very carefully at the client-worker relationship. There is a tendency in some casework for workers to think that they know best; that they are the experts. This can lead, all too easily, to a way of thinking about the work that makes clients into objects to be acted upon. What is being suggested here is that social work involves actions between *subjects*.

A practice approach focuses on dialogue. It does not begin with the formulation of objectives. In *praxis* there can be no prior knowledge of the right means by which we realize the end in a situation. This does not mean we enter situations without any idea of what the possible outcomes may be: rather, we begin with a commitment to further well-being and bring into play various ideas and images so that we may come to an initial understanding of the task involved.

The end is worked out when considering the means appropriate to a particular situation (Bernstein, 1983, p. 147). As we think about what we want to achieve, we alter the way we might achieve that. As we think about the way we might go about something, what we might aim at alters. There is a continual interplay between ends and means. Along with this has to be an openness to alternative ideas, and a search for truth. We inform this process with our commitments. When workers enter into conversations with clients with set objectives in terms of the outcomes they would like to see in the person, they tend to deny the possibility of dialogue. It is a situation parallelled in manager-worker relationships, as Jennifer Lapompe suggests in Chapter 10. In these circumstances we are not likely to be open to what the other person is saying, or to the possible truth in their words and actions.

Through conversation we begin to work out what might be the right action for the situation. We listen and reflect on what we hear. At the same time we call upon principles, such as the client's right to self-determination. Such a concern would have to be brought into engagement with other concerns. For example, if we were working with a statutory framework in a child protection agency, our duty is to ensure a child's protection, and to promote his or her physical, emotional and intellectual health and development (Department of Health, 1988, p. 10). In this way we search for what might be the most appropriate action for the situation. The problem in areas such as this is that it is all too easy to slip unthinkingly into routines or set procedures. We go by book, rather than engage with the situation and with the people involved. There are also pressures to achieve tasks and to complete the daily round.

An agenda for reflection

In this we can see a considerable agenda for the education of social workers (see Jeffs and Smith, 1990, pp. 124–43). Those approaches which centre on the gaining of skills and techniques will simply not do. Reflective practice involves workers building and testing theories. It entails cultivating judgment, commitment to certain ideals and the construction of a repertoire of ideas, images and patterns. Above all, it requires us to be open to what others are saying.

> Central to this process is our identity as workers. We have to begin to understand ourselves as intellectuals. Be a good craftsman: avoid any rigid set of procedures. Above all, seek to develop and to use the sociological imagination. Avoid the fetishism of method and technique. Urge the rehabilitation of the unpretentious intellectual craftsman, and try to become such a craftsman yourself. Let every man be his own methodologist; let every man be his own theorist; let theory and method again become part of the practice of a craft. (Mills, 1959, pp. 245–6)

This is the task taken up by workers in the following chapters. It is one we hope you will also take up or reaffirm in these troubled times for social work.

Questions for consideration

1 As workers you will have certain ideas about what makes for human
   well-being and happiness. What things do you think are especially
   important if people are to flourish?
2 Think back over the courses and training programmes you have experienced or know. To what extent are they based on the idea that people
   need 'theory' which can then be applied to the practice situation?
3 Reflection involves returning to experiences, attending to feelings
   and evaluating experience. Think of a recent situation where you
   have had to reflect on an experience: did these things happen?
4 Think about a situation where you have had uncomfortable or negative feelings about your practice: anger, or boredom perhaps. How
   have you dealt with these at the time and when you later reflected on
   your experience?
5 To what extent do your supervision or tutorial sessions focus on
   'solving' a casework problem rather than attending to your thoughts,
   feelings and actions?
6 How much choice do you think you have in how you practice?

References

Argyris, C. and D. Schön (1974) *Theory into Practice. Increasing Professional Effectiveness*. San Francisco: Jossey-Bass.
Audit Commission (1992) *The Community Revolution: Personal Social Services and Community Care*, London: HMSO.
Bernstein, R. J. (1983) *Beyond Objectivism and Relativism. Science, Hermeneutics and Praxis*. Oxford: Blackwell.
Biestek, F. S. (1961) *The Casework Relationship*. London: Unwin University Books.
Boud, D., R. Keogh and D. Walker (1985) 'What is reflection in learning?', in D. Boud, R. Keogh and D. Walker (eds), *Reflection. Turning Experience into Learning*. London: Kogan Page.
Buchman, M. (1990) 'How practical is contemplation in teaching?' in C. W. Day, M. Pope and P. Denicolo (eds), *Insight into Teachers' Thinking and Practice*. Basingstoke: Falmer Press.
Butler, B. and D. Elliot (1985) *Teaching and Learning for Practice*. Aldershot: Gower.
Carr, W. and S. Kemmis (1986) *Becoming Critical. Education, Knowledge and Action Research*. Lewes: Falmer.
Cochrane, A. (1993) 'Challenges from the centre' in J. Clarke (ed.) *A Crisis in Care? The Challenges to Social Work*, London: Sage.

Coulshed, V. (1988) *Social Work Practice. An Introduction.* London: Macmillan.

Danbury, H. (1986) *Teaching Practical Social Work.* Aldershot: Gower.

Davies, M. (1985) *The Essential Social Worker* (2nd edn). Aldershot: Gower.

Department of Health (1988) *Protecting Children: A Guide for Social Workers Undertaking a Comprehensive Assessment,* London: HMSO.

Department of Health and Welsh Office (1990) *Code of Practice. Mental Health Act 1983.* London: HMSO.

Dewey, J. (1933) *How We Think. A Restatement of the Relation of Reflective Thinking to the Educative Process.* Carbondale: Southern Illinois University Press.

Eisner, E. W. (1985) *The Art of Educational Evaluation: A Personal View,* Lewes: Falmer.

Geertz, C. (1983) *Local Knowledge. Further Essays in Interpretive Anthropology.* New York: Basic Books.

Henderson, P. and D. N. Thomas (1987) *Skills in Neighbourhood Work* (2nd edn). London: George Allen & Unwin.

Jeffs, T. and Smith, M. (eds) (1990) *Using Informal Education: An Alternative to Casework, Teaching and Control. Buckingham:* Open University Press.

Langan, M. (1993) 'New directions in social Work' in J. Clarke (ed) *A Crisis in Care? The Challenges to Social work,* London: Sage.

Louden, W. (1991) *Understanding Teaching. Continuity and Change in Teachers' Knowledge.* London: Cassell.

Mills, C. Wright (1959) *The Sociological Imagination* (1970 edn). Harmondsworth: Penguin.

Payne, M. (1991) *Modern Social Work Theory. A Critical Introduction.* London: Macmillan.

Pilalis, J. (1986) 'The integration of theory and practice: a re-examination of a paradoxical expectation', *British Journal of Social Work,* 16 (1), 79–96.

Pincus, A. and A. Minahan (1973) *Social Work Practice: Model and Method.* Itasca, Illinois: F. E. Peacock.

Sanjek, R. (ed.) (1990) *Fieldnotes. The Makings of Anthropology.* Ithaca: Cornell University Press.

Schön, D. A. (1983) *The Reflective Practitioner. How Professionals Think in Action.* London: Temple Smith.

Schön, D. A. (1987) *Educating the Reflective Practitioner: Towards a New Design for Teaching and Learning in the Professions.* San Francisco; Jossey-Bass.

Smith, M. K. (1994) *Local Education. Community, Conversation, Action.* Buckingham: Open University Press.

Turner, J. C. (1987) *Rediscovering the Social Group. A Self-categorization Theory.* Oxford: Blackwell.

Usher, R. and I. Bryant (1989) *Adult Education as Theory, Practice and Research. The Captive Triangle.* London: Routledge.

Usher, R. S. (1989) 'Locating adult education in the practical', in B. P. Bright (ed.), *Theory and Practice in the Study of Adult Education. The Epistemological Debate.* London: Routledge.

2

Teamworking

VAL CHAPMAN

Working in a team is a taken-for-granted feature of social work life. From the onset of training workers are made aware that they are entering an activity that demands collaboration with colleagues in their own agencies, with those employed in other helping professions, with clients and the community. Students are often assessed to ascertain how well they work with and alongside others; candidates for jobs as to how well they will fit into the team. Many workers see a happy and friendly team as a high priority, as essential for the effective delivery of a service and job satisfaction. In contrast unhappy workers will often complain that theirs is not a 'real team'.

Most discussions of social work teams are accounts of what they ought to be like rather than what they are. By contrast, Val Chapman's account is grounded in the day-to-day realities of team life. The chapter does not set out to offer models of teamwork or theoretical frameworks, but rather to convey a sense of the dynamics and experiences of working in a team. At one level it is the story of a team created, like so many others, after a departmental re-organization that few understood or wanted. At another level it provides a reflective account of the advantages and costs to the individual of working closely with others. What emerges is an indication of the ways in which teams can work even in less than ideal circumstances.

In telling the story of her team Val Chapman shows that the difference between a group of staff who have been drawn together for organizational convenience and a 'real team' is very complex. There appears to be no sharp division between the two, but rather a set of continuing processes. In this real, rather than ideal, account we see workers as active participants attempting to shape their working relationships into their own vision of a team. We see how physical space and resources can influence colleague relationships in both positive and negative ways. The contrasts and connections between formal meetings and informal office talk are explored. Val Chapman's critical comments about team-building exercises will find many friends but may also conflict with the beliefs of some readers. Her views will undoubtedly stimulate discussion.

Importantly the chapter recognizes the effect of a team's obligation to relate to outside groups, including management, and to incorporate within it passing individuals such as students. All of these are shown to be important in shaping team boundaries and identities. Val indicates that gender, race, class and religion are significant in our experience of team life. All of us will be able to identify and explore other sets of dynamics which have influenced our own teams.

Val writes from the perspective of team leader and provides an insight into the various demands that are made of those in this role. The questions posed at the end of her piece are only a few of the many which this chapter raises.

* * *

The beginning

In May 1988, when our Social Services Department was re-organized and restructured, large notices appeared on the office walls, quoting from Caius Petronius (AD 66):

> we trained hard, but it seemed that every time we were beginning to form up into teams we would be re-organized. I was to learn later in life that we tend to meet any new situation by re-organizing, and a wonderful method it can be for creating the illusion of progress while producing confusion, inefficiency and demoralization.

Meant as a wry comment, it reflected the feelings of many at the time: the fear of change, disappointment, anger, resentment, mistrust of management motives and the idealization of how we did things before. Teams were reconstructed and workers saw this as management taking the opportunity, under the cloak of restructuring, to split up 'activists' or those who did not 'toe the management line'. Management's stated objective was to balance skills, knowledge and experience across teams; the hidden agenda being to separate unhealthy, and in their view 'dysfunctional' cliques. Despite the negative feelings about re-organization, some workers were able to admit what they had not been able to previously: 'The team wasn't a good place to be sometimes, feelings weren't dealt with; I feel free in some ways now' (team member); whilst those who had been left outside established cliques felt some satisfaction: 'Well, they'll know now how it feels to be outside the group, and to be on your own' (team member).

Despite these feelings no one challenged the assumption that 'team is best' although, as Brieland, Briggs and Levenberger (1973) have highlighted, the emergence of the social work team concept occurred against a background of little research, an absence of conceptual models and few studies of effectiveness. The process of teamworking began, in a climate of leftover feelings about re-organization. As a newly forming team, we had some advantages. First, there was agreement on the task, even though it had been organizationally identified, 'to provide a social work service to a defined client group in a defined geographical area'. Second, there was a desire to offer this service according to a patch-based community development structure, aimed at demystifying social work and improving the lives of the individual and the community. Third, we shared a belief that we could have some influence on the recruitment and selection of new team members. To be able to choose team members for compatibility of personality, and to balance existing skills and knowledge while at the same time aiding team function and development was something we all thought important. The reality was less than we hoped for, but this was partly because of poorly developed recruitment and selection methods within the organization, which relied on a lengthy interview without team involvement, and also because staff who needed to be accommodated within the re-organization process were 'slotted-in' to teams with no say. The irony did not escape us that both factors could lead to imbalance, cliques and dysfunction (the problems re-organization had purported to address); this reinforced the feelings of helplessness in the face of management.

Finally, a group of eight people came together: a team leader, five social workers, a family aide and an under-fives adviser, later to be supplemented by a part-time team clerk. The team is a mixture of qualified and unqualified workers, at various levels of development and competency, consisting of two men and seven women. The word 'team' was at first being used in a manner suggested by Payne to describe 'not only where a team (whatever it is) exists but also where someone hopes it does, or wishes it would' (Payne, 1982).

How we work

Despite arguments contained within various reports, notably Seebohm (1968) and Barclay (1982), that accessible area teams 'out in the community' are especially well placed to engage in community development and preventive work, our team is housed in a small corner of the Civic Centre, a large complex housing various local authority departments.

Although reasonably accessible to the public, the office is not particularly welcoming or comfortable and does not lend itself to confidentiality. The duty desk is visible and conversation is audible to the public via the reception window; the reception area is itself shared with members of the public requiring travel permits. Two adjacent windows ensure everyone in the waiting area is able to identity who is and who is not a social work client.

The team area is badly lit and enjoys little natural light. The desks can only be placed at angles which are not conducive to a feeling of 'team togetherness'. There is no way the desks can be moved as the arrangements were pre-planned to maximize the use of space, a situation that has worsened considerably since the increase in staff employed to administer revenue collection. The open-plan design, broken up only by small screens, gives little opportunity for quiet work, and the telephone system even less for confidentiality. The difficulties of the reception duty desk, the seating arrangements, and the lack of privacy and confidentiality are all constant issues among the team. We feel we have little power to change these, despite various attempts to do so. In spite of the limitations of the seating, it is the place where most of the informal team support happens. Most telephone conversations are overheard and advice can be sought on the spot; where people are seen to be writing reports or assessments, information will be volunteered, requested and exchanged. One cup of coffee usually means four more for the rest of the team, and work will cease for a short time for social chat and an exchange of opinions. Unhappy or worried faces will be noted and support offered, help volunteered. The team may complain about lack of privacy or quiet, but it is usually only desperation regarding a deadline for a report that will lead an individual to retreat to the privacy of a meeting room with a closed door. It is a fact of social work life that a lot of written work is taken home to be completed or caught up on. Mainly this is due to overwork, but it is also partly the result of not being assertive enough to seek a private place.

More formal support occurs during team meetings. A weekly meeting provides a necessary service for the team as well as the organization. This sometimes feels like a strange mixture. We try to balance this by going through the business agenda first. This will usually comprise referrals and allocations, correspondence, information sharing and the identification of issues that need to be taken up or clarified. Allocation of work is likely to be the major piece of business, and this is done as democratically as possible. All referrals will be read and discussed among the team, and 'bids' will be made for specific ones on the basis of interest in a particular area of work, as an aid to professional development or simply because the caseload of a member is lower than average: 'I suppose I'd better take it, I've just closed a couple of cases.' Allocation is probably the area where most of the games that occur in teams are played, the most obvious one being 'avoidance by silence'. A referral will be discussed and no bid will be made. The game begins. Which worker will give in first and volunteer to take it on? This is usually the most accommodating member of the team, embarrassed by the silence; or the least confident member who will give way under the group pressure. This game is often used as a form of regulation by the majority who may identify one or more team members as not carrying a fair balance of the work, but who do not feel able to say so openly within the group. This could lead to damaging confrontation; instead, we are trying to ensure a fairer method of distribution of work by looking at a team-devised caseload weighting system. Team members are aware that the ultimate sanction in allocation can come from the team leader. From an awareness of workload the team leader will sometimes allocate without a bid being made. Usually before this happens the referral will be taken by someone on the basis of 'I'll take it; you'd probably give it to me anyway'! While this democratic method of allocation can work, it does (as already noted) lend itself to group games. These may be minimized within a fairminded co-operative team capable of applying group pressure to provide checks and balances or by a team leader who seeks fairness and consistency. In our district it is also aided by a workable number of referrals.

Child protection referrals are dealt with in a different manner. All these are subject to a joint investigation, either by two team members or a team member and a member of the Police Child Protection Unit. Alleged sexual abuse is always investigated in conjunction with the Police Child Protection Unit. While procedures dictate that investigations should be carried out by a qualified level three social worker, this does not always happen due to pressure of work, sickness and holidays. Management passively sanction this. These investigations are often where workers feel most vulnerable and accountable, and where teamwork and team support are most likely to be demonstrated. Team members will work together without instruction but in a structured way to identify and divide tasks, according to agency procedures and guidelines; offer practical support and advice; cover appointments and duty; and wait around the office after hours for the return of the investigating team members to offer sympathy, support and advice.

The rest of the team business will take place following referrals and allocations. This involves sharing information, reporting back from training courses, discussing books or articles of interest and looking at where the team is and how it should develop. The team meeting can be the forum where informal team-building processes happen, as relationships are formed, trust is built up, skills developed and shared issues tackled, as well as being an opportunity for the exchange of support and advice. It can be the forum which breeds the beginning of a team identity, both for positive and negative reasons. In the beginning we huddled together for protection and support, but as time has gone on our dependency on each other has become more of an expression of the group of staff developing into a real team.

In retrospect it is possible to see that the team underwent Tuckman's (1965) four processes of team development: that is, forming, storming (fighting over territory in the group), norming (coming to general agreement about how the group should work) and performing (getting on with work-sharing without worrying too much about relationships in the group). Unresolved issues regarding relationships do still exist within the team, but there is now a tacit agreement that exploring them is unnecessary. It is felt that unless they affect the work of the team, there is no point in hurting feelings and causing embarrassment. I have worked in teams where relationship difficulties existed, games were played at every team meeting, and mature people fled the room sobbing to lock themselves in the toilet. A student at the time, I was often the one left to coax them out, as no one else was speaking to each other, or the one who provided, literally 'the shoulder to cry on'. I suppose these experiences have influenced my present attitude of avoiding confrontation until every other method or tactic has been tried; others will have their own reasons and rationale. I am aware that team problems can, and do, exist, and that current team members may try to use students or new team members as allies, or to win points in the games.

Formalized team-building and team development have not had the effect management might have wished to achieve. We have been resistant to team-building agendas which lacked clarity and to crudely developed methods which do not appear to relate to the actual working experience. These exercises ignore the point that most development is self-regulated, and people cannot be forced into changing attitudes. I did not see the point as a student of kneeling on the classroom floor to complete a team jigsaw of a parrot, and neither do I see the point as a child protection worker in designing a chocolate bar wrapper; I am sure many do. Trust games may raise a laugh while a blindfolded colleague falls trustingly into the outstretched arms of colleagues; no one I know relates it to real-life working situations. The nuclear shelter game, when played by the team, threw out the social workers as the second to go. I saw this as healthy criticism as to the value of a social worker in a post-nuclear war bunker; management saw it in different terms, and the team was labelled unco-operative and destructive of team-building programmes. It may be seen as a facile view, but our experience in building a team has been that progress has flowed from the everyday working situation, group activities, shared experiences and the need for support and protection. The team see themselves as 'built' as necessary to complete the task. Colleagues support one another in some way every working day (for example, in covering duty, supervised accesses and help in preparing reports). Imposed team-building has been seen as destructive rather constructive. This is not to say we believe the process of team-building and development is automatic, or that the team is unaware of dysfunctional areas. However, unless dysfunction is crippling, small difficulties can be silently acknowledged and set aside. Confrontation is not seen as necessary. Every issue does not have to be put on the table, and people do not feel they need to share intimacies or bare their souls to construct a team. The team view is that they function at an acceptable level of adequacy and fulfil the task. We do work as a team and we support each other. One member described their experience of the team like this: 'I can usually get duty cover or a supervised access done and I do it for others; I go to the team for advice and they come to me. I don't feel I have to love them all to get it.'

Of course, relationships within teams can and do go wrong. If major issues are not worked through or are acknowledged they can cause problems and stultify development. In an area of major dysfunction the team may be unable to tackle or solve the issue themselves and require outside guidance or direction (see Woodcock 1979). Our experience has been that in the main we get by and the team is mostly a supportive, enjoyable place to be. It is to the team that individuals turn when work becomes too awful, experiences too harrowing and feelings confused. This support is also offered individually via informal contact and formal supervision with the team leader. I do not intend to develop this further here, as the chapter is about being part of a team. I would only wish to point out that individual supervision involving examination of caseloads and identification of the need for areas of personal and professional development supplement the work of the team. In addition to support from colleagues and informal supervision, team members also acknowledge support from spouses, partners, family and friends, with whom it is sometimes felt safer to discuss the 'feelings' aspect of the job. Expressing feelings is perhaps seen as weakness, and succumbing to them a sign of failure! Teams working in the field of child physical and sexual abuse are vulnerable to feelings of depression, horror and repugnance regarding some of the abuses they have to deal with. These occur however well-equipped we may have considered ourselves to face such feelings. The team would appear to be the ideal place to come to terms with these, but this seems at present (for us at least) to be too threatening a forum. Some local authorities have begun to address this problem by retaining professional counsellors on a consultancy basis. This approach, it is argued, enables the confidentiality of the referral to be maintained. Our team is sceptical of the confidentiality offered and the value that this service might provide.

I would now like to explore briefly some areas which, while not involving direct team work, impinge on team relationships.

The duty system

The duty arrangement entails each social worker being part of the duty rota; there are three teams in the District, two child-care teams and the health and welfare team. The duty system is possibly the only area of contact between the child-care and health and welfare teams, apart from occasional joint training events. Consequently, while we operate a general duty system, workloads are not generic, resulting in little knowledge of each other's roles and specialist skills. The health and welfare team are seen as being professionals somewhat apart from us. Our relationship with the other child-care team is of a mixed nature. Mutual help and support occurs, but there is a clear and distinct separation of responsibilities and an element of competitiveness. Requests for duty cover will initially be made within one's own team, then to the other child-care team, and only in the last instance to the health and welfare team. While acknowledging the importance of a duty system as often the first point of contact between client and agency, duty is not seen as a priority. Team members can forget they have a duty day, arrive late, or make external appointments. While these actions are normally treated with tolerance by the team it can occasionally develop into an area of friction where people are seen to be letting down the collective. This lack of commitment to, and prioritization of, the duty system is intermittently the subject of management scrutiny and it is mainly child-care teams who are the most culpable. Students are occasionally over, or inappropriately, used for duty cover, as well as for transport.

Students

I have mentioned above the inappropriate use of students, particularly for duty work and transport. Not wishing to frighten off prospective students, I would like to highlight the team approach to student placements. Proposed placements are discussed at team meetings, and agreements reached regarding support and supervision. All team members will involve students in special activities, visits to establishments, community development work and, where possible, client contact. Ideally the student will meet the team before the placement starts, and will be invited to convey their particular interests or training needs. It is not unknown, however, for a student to arrive on placement without any prior knowledge of the team, its specializations or expertise. Students have also arrived during the practice teacher's prolonged absence; the team worked hard to minimize the trauma of this! Students are formally welcomed at team meetings and encouraged to attend these as regularly as possible and to become participants rather than observers. Students are often a stimulating presence who provoke re-examination of current practices in the light of new teaching and theory. They are also useful in taking on new work or pieces of work from current caseloads that may benefit from more intensive input or a fresh look at the situation. To benefit fully from their placements students need a preparation which includes some knowledge of group dynamics and processes, plus the confidence and assertiveness to enable them to resist being drawn into games or collusive relationships within teams. A sense of humour is a real asset!

Comings and goings

The introduction of new workers into our team was like so many others, being until recently unstructured and *ad hoc*. Now there is a formal induction process for new workers, and conscious attempts are made to involve workers in team gatherings prior to the official starting date. Our team social life is mainly restricted to 'office hours' with team lunches, birthdays marked by cakes at the team meeting and frequent exchanges of gossip or complaints about workload and management. Natural good humour and banter are commonplace, with the inevitable running jokes about who is always late, who never makes the tea and who needs three desks to work on. We have a 'quote of the week' board on which particular *bon mots*, witticisms or sarcasms are written. These are small rituals which help establish and maintain our team boundary and identity. Endings are marked formally, with presentations done by higher management, and less formally by team lunches and drinks. Usually people are careful not to get drunk enough to carry out the declared intent 'to tell them all what I think of them when I leave'. Everyone promises to keep in touch. Usually, no one does.

Relationships with management

Team relationships with management remain of a 'them and us' type. There is distrust of management's motives and a feeling that inadequate acknowledgment is made regarding our worth, particularly concerning our preventive work. Workers see things 'done to' them by management, with power imposed from above. They feel that management lacks understanding of the stress of face-to-face work, and is obsessed with statistics which are seen to be used as a rationale for changing boundaries or dividing posts in order to impose unwanted change. Management controls budgets and social workers are often seen to be throwing money at problems rather than seeking long-term solutions. Lack of policy and procedures leaves social workers vulnerable. Attempts at negotiations are seen as lip service. None of the above is peculiar to our team, or unexplained. Parsloe (1981) has written of worker perceptions of their relationship to management as a displacement of the inherent anxieties of the job (p. 92). Pithouse suggested it was more a means of asserting a right to 'Cherished Autonomy' (Pithouse, 1989, p. 48). I would add to these that the perception of 'them and us' helps maintain team boundary and identity. For a fuller discussion, readers may wish to read Pithouse's Chapter 4.

Class, religion, gender and race

The team are all white and are mainly working-class people who somewhat uneasily accept the social classification acquired by our profession. There is very little to remark on regarding class/gender issues within the team except that we tend to share a common value and belief system. Race is not a high-profile issue within the team. While we agree on positive discrimination and equal opportunities, there has been no active recruitment of minority workers. The largest ethnic group in our area is Jews, who, for a variety of reasons, are not traditional users of Social Services, so there is minimal client contact with any minority ethnic group. Child protection procedures and guidelines, residential or fostering placements and assessments are limited in their application to minority groups. The team agree on the limitations of our knowledge or experience in these areas. We acknowledge the 'issues'; we try to remain aware of them in our practice; but we never address them in any comprehensive ways.

A wider team

Following restructuring, the District decided to attempt an integrated approach to service delivery, incorporating residential services. While social workers had good working relationships with individual residential care workers, the residential service was seen by the team as being somewhat second class, staffed by people with inferior qualifications. There was little understanding of roles on either side. The integrative process was initiated by means of joint training, involving the identification of common areas of interest, skills and knowledge. Although initially viewed negatively, this has been a reasonably successful integrative exercise, and one which is continued by joint Children Act training. This approach has proved a more successful method of team-building than more formal team-building training. The level of integration sought was a clearer understanding of each other's roles and the services we could provide, and this was achieved.

Readers will recognize that formalized team-building is something I have little sympathy for. Our experience is that team-building training without clear aims and agendas is more destructive than constructive. Crude, poorly developed methodology leads to disengagement and resistance. In contrast to 'quick fix' methods of team-building, the integration of the pre-school adviser, money advice worker, welfare rights worker and team clerks has been achieved slowly and after protests about confidentiality, by a process of getting to know the people personally and using them professionally.

Finally, I would like to consider the role of the team leader, which I feel to be of central importance. Team leaders, like teams, were seen by both Seebohm and Barclay to be desirable, yet neither attempted a definitive statement of the role or how it might be administered. Parsloe has commented that team leaders are in a crucial position in the Social Services:

> The quality of their leadership may be the most important single influence upon the nature of the team and the quality of the service clients receive. They link their team members to the organisation and to other agencies in the local community, and are also the bridge by which the hierarchy and other agencies influence team members. (Parsloe, 1981, p. 127)

Briel, Briggs and Levenberger (1973, p. 9) expand this definition to include professional responsibility for the team; accountability; knowledge of everyone receiving a service from the team; determining an equitable distribution of work; orientating and teaching team members, evaluating and advocating, and having the power of veto.

I have included these comments to indicate what team members might expect of their team leader and to highlight the tensions inherent in the job. The main one is often how to achieve a balance between being part of the management structure and part of a team of workers. The team, while understanding the dilemma, demands the balance be tipped in its favour. The link with management is seen as useful only in terms of facilitating the flow of information and pushing issues upwards. What the team values most is, according to its members, loyalty, honesty, openness, support and protection. Skills and knowledge are seen as useful, but less important than the aforementioned requirements. This list could equally apply to what the team leader requires from the team, and I have become, over time, more able to acknowledge that I need support from the team (see Cypher, 1982; and Cockburn, 1990).

Before drawing this chapter to a conclusion, I would like to acknowledge an absence of exploration of certain areas, notably contact with clients. This does not seem relevant to the theme of teamworking, which feels odd, as providing a service to the client is why the team exists. I have needed to remind myself throughout that this is an observation of a process and not an account of how a service is delivered, and I hope this focus has not been lost.

Conclusion

Most social workers will be part of a team, and there appears little preparation for this process. I have suggested the need for preparation and induction, particularly in understanding group processes. Writing the chapter made me take the opportunity to look at the literature available on teams and teamworking and to place our team's experience alongside research and theoretical discussions of teams. Most of the literature I have been able to find has been theoretical and conceptual in nature, which has helped to rationalize the experiences we have undergone as a team. However, very little of the literature conveys in any depth the 'feel' of being part of a team, or the personal commitment required to make one work. What I have learnt from writing the chapter is that teams can work even when not created in the ideal circumstances. At their worst, teams can be dysfunctional and disabling; at less than their best they can provide safety and support and opportunities for personal and professional development. Being part of a team can be a frightening process. Finding a place and a role is both daunting and difficult; often this process needs to be facilitated. We have learnt most by taking time out as a team and building up relationships and strengths to deal with the majority of issues that arise. Teamworking is displayed every day, rather than within artificially created training situations.

Conflicts do, and will continue to, arise. As pointed out, participation in decision-making and problem-solving does not guarantee that teams will operate without conflict, but this can be seen as a force for team development (Brieland, Briggs and Levenberger, 1973, p. 27). The consensus view of our team (allowing for sample bias and the questioner!) is that the team is working. We measure our success by the service we are able to provide, and as a team we feel that the delivery of this is improved by the pooling of the knowledge and skill available within an integrated team. Team life prepares us for working with wider teams, in multi-disciplinary and community settings, whilst knowledge and confidence in ourselves as teamworkers enhances what we are able to contribute to those wider teams. We are not in a 'perfect' state, if such a state exists. Rather, I suspect, in common with many others, we are at an intermediate stage of supportive and safe development; we are able to get by and survive, whilst offering the consumer an effective service, which is ultimately the desired goal.

While writing the chapter, I have been disappointed by the volume and quality of literature available on the subject, and the apparent dearth of up-to-date material. However, the books referenced at the end of this chapter have been interesting and thought-provoking. I particularly enjoyed the historical overview of the emergence of teams in Brieland, Briggs and Levenberger (1973) and the introduction to the Lonsdale, Webb and Briggs (1990) collection on the *ad hoc* adoption of the team approach. The Parsloe (1981) and Payne (1982) contributions are the most satisfying in terms of providing some 'human' feel of teamworking. My favourite description of teamwork appears on page 1, Chapter 1 of the Lonsdale, Webb and Briggs book: 'Team-work': A desideratum and a problem'. That just about sums it up!

Questions for consideration

1 What makes a group of staff into a team?
2 Can team problems be solved without confrontation?
3 How might a team deal with a team member who avoids a fair share of work?

4   Can you suggest a framework for introducing new members into a team? How would you take account of dynamics such as (dis)ability, gender, heterosexism and racism in this?
5   Design a team-building event that is relevant, non-threatening and understandable!

References

Barclay, P. (1982) *Social Workers: Their Role and Tasks*, Report of the Working Party. London: Bedford Square Press.

Brieland, D., T. Briggs and P. Levenberger (1973) *The Team Model of SW Practice*, Manpower Monograph No. 5, Syracuse University.

Cockburn, J. (1990) *Team Leaders and Team Managers in the Social Services.* SW Monographs, Department of Social Work. Norwich: University of East Anglia.

Cypher, J. (1982) *Team Leadership in the Social Services.* Birmingham: BASW Publications.

Lonsdale, S. A. Webb and T. Briggs (1980) *Team-work in the Personal Social Services and Health Care.* London: Croom Helm.

Parsloe, P. (1981) *Social Services Area Teams.* London: Allen & Unwin.

Payne, M. (1982) *Working in Teams.* London: Macmillan.

Pithouse, A. (1987) Social Work: The Social Organization of an Invisible Trade. Aldershot: Gower.

Pithouse, A. (1989) 'Guardian of Autonomy: Work Orientations in a Social Work Office', in P. Carter, T. Jeffs and M. Smith (eds), *Year Book of Social Work and Social Welfare.* Milton Keynes, Open University Press.

Seebohm, F. (1968) *Report of the Committee on Local Authority and Allied Personal Social Services.* London: HMSO.

Tuckman, B. W. (1965) 'Developments in Small Groups', *Psychological Bulletin*, 63 (b), 384–99.

Woodcock, M. (1979) *Team Development Manual.* Aldershot: Gower.

3

Records and Record Keeping

PATSY LITTLE

Record keeping is viewed by many workers as at best a necessary evil, something that has to be fitted into spare moments snatched from what are perceived as more important tasks. Even most students at the onset of their professional lives are encouraged into this view. The skills and attributes that are prioritized and valued rarely include the need to undertake effective recording. Such work is seen as bureaucratic rather than creative; something that in an ideal world might somehow be delegated to a clerk or administrative assistant.

At the beginning of her professional life Patsy Little shared this view. Instead of going along with the dominant belief she decided to confront it. Through an interrogation of her own practice she shows us how she came to re-assess the purpose and role of recording. Ultimately she came to regard it as a meaningful and essential aspect of professional thinking, as a means by which reflection upon practice might become part of the daily life of each and every social worker.

The chapter is in itself an example of the systematic, reflective and questioning process which useful recording should entail. Patsy Little works carefully and honestly through the basic questions of why record; what to record; how to record; and what use are records. Her account is undoubtedly shaped by her particular work in a youth justice centre, where major parts of her work involve challenging attitudes and behaviour. The examples which she gives show how her method of recording is geared to that end. Workers in other settings may well want to ask whether, and how, their recording addresses what has been identified as the fundamental purpose of their work with clients, or whether it is geared only to organizational convenience and convention.

At each point the chapter shows that recording is simultaneously technical and creative. Most of us will be impressed by just how readable and interesting Patsy's case records are. This is clearly a product of recording being central to her work, not something tacked on as an afterthought. But this quality of writing is something she has clearly developed over time. Her commitment to recording has grown not simply as a matter of principle but, as she has demonstrated to herself and to others (including her clients), shows how useful writing things down can be. Many of us will be prompted to reflect on how the usefulness and accessibility of our own records can be enhanced.

As well as being a technical and potentially creative activity, recording also raises some key ethical questions. The most obvious one relates to confidentiality. Patsy Little's discussion about confidentiality shows that this is an issue which must be confronted anew in each setting. There are no simple rules.

This thorough account of recording shows the influence of workers' own feelings, values and beliefs on their work with clients. In striving for objectivity, which Patsy sees as important, it will be clear that workers need to explore their own subjective judgments. In some settings differences between workers and clients (for example, of race, gender and class) will be key dimensions of this reflection. Developing a careful recording system is one way in which these explorations can be facilitated.

* * *

I have been recording my work as a matter of routine for the past four years.

Prior to my training, I simply did not do it, or place any particular value on it, apart from perhaps recording what I judged to be significant events on an *ad hoc* basis. On reflection, I must own that I considered the subject of recording dry and, akin to statistics, to be avoided like the plague! This chapter is not intended to give guidance on how the task should be accomplished; neither indeed do I make the assumption that the way in which I record would be suitable for other workers. My aim is to illustrate what I have found to be the advantages and pitfalls, both practical and theoretical, of recording and record keeping.

I must begin by making clear what I mean by recording. I have given this considerable thought. By recording I mean a systematic account of transactions between myself (and other workers in the agency) and particular client(s). Such an account must also fulfil certain criteria:

(a) it must be regularly carried out as a matter of normal working practice;
(b) it must of some use;
(c) it should be succinct and therefore manageable in terms of 'reading and writing time';
(d) it should be an account based on evidence rather than assumption, and contain information appropriate to the primary task of the agency;
(e) it should be readable for both worker(s) and client(s) in terms of legibility and language use.

Why record in the first place?

I record for two reasons.

First, I believe that it would be impossible to work effectively unless I did so. This conviction developed during my training, which demanded three years' study, relating theory to working practice, using my recordings as a basis for assignments, seminars and during supervision. This discipline did not come easily. However, after a struggle, recording has become an integral part of my work. I believe this more purposeful style must also be of significant benefit to the client(s) in terms of the service they receive.

Second, I record certain information because I am required to do so as part of my job. Recording in my agency falls into three main types: basic statistical information routinely gathered on each client; individual casenotes describing transactions between client and worker; separate recordings relating to groupwork. Before explaining how this seemingly onerous task is undertaken, it may be helpful to examine the reasons for recording in more detail.

For the client

Through a recording of attendances, clients are able to ascertain how many sessions they have completed. A young person may be required by the court to attend the project 'up to a maximum of 90 days'. Failure to comply could constitute a breach of the supervision order. Clients want to know how many sessions are left, particularly as an incentive at the beginning of their programme, and again when it is drawing to its close.

> I spent almost one hour talking with Dawn. After looking at her file, we saw that she has only twenty sessions to complete. Together we decided how to gradually decrease the sessions, incorporating her home tuition and work experience into the plan. Dawn says she now feels more confident about her impending review, scheduled for Thursday.

These sessional records illustrate the progress made by clients regarding their offending behaviour, and also achievements and changes in their lives generally, such as those concerning school attendance, gaining employment, relationships and accommodation.

> David told me that he has got himself a job in the chicken factory. He says he will be able to cope with the shiftwork, and transport is not a problem as he will be picked up by the factory bus. I explained that we normally deduct two additional sessions per week for every full week's work he does. In addition, I emphasised that David will still be expected to attend the evening 'Focus on Offending' group, for which one session will also be deducted from his requirement. I said David had done well to get himself a job.

Frequently, events only become significant with hindsight, and it is through recording that both worker and client are able to recognize and analyse these changes.

> Looking back, Scott said that he could see that the biggest change for him was when he moved out of home and into his bedsit. Scott now gets on much better with his Dad, and although he still has difficulty managing money, Scott is really enjoying his independence. Scott says he feels more worried now about the idea of 'going down' and wants to keep out of trouble.

For me as worker

Systematic recordings enable both client and worker to gain visual evidence of developments. Through recording I am able to gain an overall picture of work with a particular individual or group, and can observe how the interventions I have made build upon each other and evaluate the cumulative effect.

> I congratulated Dawn on her performance in the review meeting. I pointed out to her that when she first came to the project I had noted that she seemed unable to look anyone in the face, and was unwilling to take part in any of the meetings to discuss her future. I reminded Dawn that she had found it impossible to sit in the room for more than about ten minutes, on the occasions when she did decide to try and take part. I emphasised her achievement in sitting through the whole meeting, in such a large group, and the importance of the comments she had made. We spoke about the possible reasons for this progress.

Similarly, in the counselling situation, it is important to be able to assess how much the client has 'moved on' during the process, as well as to examine my own performance. So much can emerge from one hour's counselling that it would be impossible to remember it all without making some notes.

Recordings provide written evidence of my performance as a worker, which can be used as a basis for further analysis, enabling me to determine the effectiveness of my interventions, and to identify alternative ways of working in the future: 'All the members seemed to have difficulty in answering the question about what they hoped to gain from the group. I realised that in future we would have to do some work on expectations in the initial group session, along with establishing boundaries and formulating the group contract'.

By keeping records, I am able to monitor my practice. The act of writing something down often crystallizes a particular problem or issue, or enables me to see where a particular piece of work has not achieved its objective. The cultivation of this skill is an essential contribution to my professional development. Through this process I can identify my strengths and weaknesses, and areas in which I could benefit from further training.

The three reasons usually cited for making recordings are to benefit service delivery, to enable professional development and to supply data for research. As far as this last is concerned, statistics of clients are gathered by our project and collated at head office. These could indicate offending rates, sentencing trends, types of offences, or age/sex ratios of clients. This system provides useful data for research into juvenile offending and assists in enhancing the credibility of similar community-based schemes. At a national level, data supplied by individual projects can influence government policy through consultative committees and research papers. Equally, local data may assist in the formulation of national or regional agency policy.

What to record?

The majority of our clients are referred via the youth court and will become the subject of a supervision order. Within the justice system, reports play a significant part. Reports from a variety of agencies, including an assessment by ourselves, may be offered to the magistrates to assist them in deciding the most *suitable* method of disposal. Once allocated to our agency, we employ four methods of working with clients, and these must also therefore form the basis of our recordings. In common with the methods, it is important that the recordings are client-centred rather than focusing on the actions or feelings of the worker, although these will be included as appropriate. Let us continue by examining what is recorded for each of our methods of working.

One-to-one work. On referral, each young person is allocated a keyworker who is responsible for organizing the programme of work, maintaining records, liaising with the supervising officer and writing reports. Clients will compile an 'Offending History' with their keyworker. This gives valuable information about patterns of offending, reactions from family and school and individual circumstances which may have led to the offending; it also provides a point from which to start work. Details about family, friends, hobbies, employment and schooling will also be recorded.

After these initial information-gathering exercises, the counselling begins. It is not normal practice to take notes during the session. I record what seem to be the most significant facts, issues and emotions expressed by the client at each meeting. The important point to recognize for this method of working is that it is clients who set the agenda in the sense that they decide what is discussed, providing it focuses on themselves as individuals. The aim is to enable clients to work on their problems themselves.

The counsellor works from where clients are now, at their pace, and strives to be non-judgmental. My recordings should reflect this.

> Initially, Tracy seemed rather subdued. There was a very long silence. Suddenly, she blurted out that she had completely changed her mind about 'going away' next week even though all the arrangements have been made. Tracy said she would not stay at the children's home and would 'do a runner' if she was sent there. Tracy said she felt she was being sent away as a punishment.

Groupwork. 'Focus on Offending' groups form a major component of our work, and it is essential that these sessions are adequately recorded.

Each session is planned in advance and concentrates on a particular theme, but is also structured to encourage maximum input from group members. The plan for the session is recorded, and workers are clear about who will facilitate which exercise or topic. The recording will include what roles seem to be emerging, how the group tackled the task, group processes and dynamics, the general 'feel' of the session plus notes of the main points of discussion.

> Mark was clearly in the role of scapegoat. He made himself particularly vulnerable to this by giving inappropriate answers during the session and also by taking the mickey out of the responses given by other group members. Andy called Mark a 'pratt' and Wayne also joined in making disparaging remarks although he has only met Mark on two previous occasions.

More detailed notes of clients' behaviour and contributions during groupwork sessions are recorded in their individual folders, separate from the 'group recording', and this may form a basis for future work.

> I spoke to Mark about his performance at this week's evening group. I asked how it felt to be continually 'got at' by other group members. Mark said he didn't care. I said that the reason could be that he continually took the mickey out of their responses, and asked if Mark took the role of joker in school. Mark said he did and that his classmates seemed to find it funny. Mark admitted he was finding it very difficult to cope with the different reaction from this group.

Activity groups. These recordings reflect individual progress, not simply in terms of being 'good at' the activity, but reinforcing any small achievement and noting any particular aptitude or enthusiasm. Activities include a variety of sports, games, group outings and camping trips. Personality traits, such as inability to function as part of a team, over-competitiveness, emotional reactions and ability to carry out instructions, are recorded. These provide material to work on, either in the feedback session after the activity or on a one-to-one basis at another time.

The vocal players seemed dominant. Kevin and Gareth were shouting instructions. Terry seemed to be playing for fun. It seemed another hierarchy was emerging – based on individuals' ability to play football and score goals, rather than on acquired status from the project. Kevin seemed conscious that his role as leader was diminished by John, who was the best footballer.

Practical work. There is also a community service element to the programme. The aim of these sessions is to acquire practical skills while making reparation to the community in some way for the offence. Tasks including gardening, painting and decorating, and basic woodwork. Recordings concentrate on clients' general ability, skills possessed and skills acquired. These recordings are more 'task-related' in that they concentrate on 'jobs done'. There is some comment on general attitude and behaviour.

* * *

In addition to the methods of working, other aspects of face-to-face work are also recorded, such as critical incidents and home visits. Critical incidents may occur at any time, in any setting, and while employing any of the methods mentioned above. By a 'critical incident' I mean one which would seem to be significant, either to client, worker or agency. I record the incident as fully as possible, as in the extract of a recording quoted below.

Chris attended the group as usual. We had decided to play a board game focusing on alcohol abuse instead of the usual exercise and discussion format. Chris seemed very tense and quiet during the initial setting out of the game and explanations of how to play. He joined in quite well for the first couple of rounds, but then came to a point where he had to read a card out loud. Chris picked up the card and began to read, obviously finding it really difficult. One of the girls began to giggle. Chris looked as though he wanted to hit her, he was very white and his fists were clenched. Suddenly, he grabbed the small table with the game on it and turned it upside down. The game, cards and counters all went flying. Chris swore, turned and stormed out of the room, slamming the door. For the first time, I realised that Chris could hardly read.

Events such as this are frequently 'turning points' in our work, and are situations where considerable progress may be made, often in a comparatively short space of time.

Home visits are recorded in summary form in the client's running record. Detailed information may include whether or not the client was punctual, observations of changes in appearance or circumstances.

I called for Sarah at home as arranged. She did not answer the door for a long time. Eventually she opened the door and let me in. The house was very untidy and smelt of stale cigarettes. All the curtains were closed so it was quite dark. Sarah's clothes were dirty and crumpled and her hair was greasy. I thought she looked ill.

All the above are necessary for effective work with clients, but in addition I need to record for a number of other purposes.

Time allocation. I keep a weekly diary noting how I use my time, outlining the main events, which tasks have been achieved and which have yet to be completed. The aim is to achieve a balance between administrative and face-to-face work. This does not always go to plan, but it is important for me to be aware of how much time I allocate to each individual: is one client getting a lot of my time, and if so, is it appropriate? What work have I been unable to do with one client as a result of the way I prioritized my time with another? Because of our rural location, a significant proportion of time is taken up with travel, transporting clients and travelling to appointments. These journeys are also recorded. I compile the diary in summative form at the end of each week, day-by-day. This diary focuses on me as a worker.

Team meetings and supervision sessions. These are recorded, on separate sheets, and filed with my weekly diary. I record decisions taken, objectives set and reached, and suggestions for future action. I note all material directly relevant to myself as a worker, or to clients for whom I am keyworker. These notes are used to assist me in planning my work, and as a reminder of the tasks I have undertaken to complete.

Meetings such as case conferences, reviews and planning meetings are minuted and the record filed in the individual client's folder.

How I carry out the task

There is no single way to carry out the task of recording. For example, regarding casenotes, the bulk of the material is contained in clients' individual folders. At the front of each is a grid showing number of attendances and a referral form giving basic statistical information including antecedents, sentence details and name of the supervising officer. It also includes medical and parental consent forms. The remainder of the case-folder is divided into four sections, as outlined below.

Running record. This forms the main log of our work. Notes are made in summative form detailing what the worker perceives to be the significant events or issues from each session. I also record my own thoughts and feelings, where appropriate, and notes of future objectives. These notes are kept daily, or as soon as possible after the event, ideally within 24 hours. Notes are handwritten initially, then typed up at a later date by the secretary. This running record also contains recordings of any 'critical incidents'. The contract formulated at the 'Offending Group' is signed and kept in the client's folder, along with any written exercises, assessment and evaluation forms completed by the client.

Correspondence. This includes copies of letters written concerning the client by the project or received by us. This includes clients' appointments with other agencies. Clients who fail to attend the project without good reason may end up facing breach proceedings. Our system for this begins with a warning in letter form. Expected sessional attendances at the project are confirmed in writing.

Assessment, reviews, personal documentation, care orders, social enquiry reports. This section contains 'official' documents written by other agencies regarding the client, and copies of any court or assessment reports written by ourselves. Clients will have seen the majority of the information stored here at some time, most commonly during a court appearance.

Closed (material in this section to be authorized by a senior officer). This section is not greatly used in our project, as our records focus on current work with a client, rather than past history. However, any documents marked 'strictly confidential' would be stored here (for example, minutes from case conferences where the client was excluded, child protection meetings and confidential medical reports).

A daily office diary is also kept in which workers note down appointments, meetings and a rota for picking up clients. A skeleton timetable for the week, decided at the team meeting, is entered in the diary. In a small staff team such as ours, it is important that we are aware of each other's schedules in order to maintain regular contact with our clients, attend meetings and cover the youth court and office duty.

Recordings are kept in locked cabinets in the office, which is alarmed out of hours. This is essential because of the sensitive nature of the material stored. Confidentiality must be maintained, particularly as we work with young offenders, whose court appearances are not usually made public. The files contain detailed information concerning many aspects of individual clients' circumstances, which are regarded as strictly confidential.

Recording methods

I aim to keep recordings manageable in length and so usually use a summative form, except for a 'critical incident' where a more detailed record is required. I endeavour to use a method appropriate to the material. Methods include the critical incident technique, which involves asking myself a predetermined set of questions about the incident, recording the answers and then identifying a course of action and the resources I will need to carry it out. Process recordings are detailed and focus on the process of work done, rather than what happened as a result. Process recordings contain interpretation and descriptions of feelings, and are essentially a study tool.

I also employ the descriptive account recording method which provides an account of what occurred, some analysis, and a plan for future action within a particular format: the page is divided into two columns, so that the account of events is separate from the analysis. This recording concludes with a brief assessment and action plan.

I also record in the form of minutes and diaries.

For me, the criterion is that the method should be adequate for its usage. There should be a distinction between fact and assumption or hypothesis, which should be clearly stated. I aim for 'objectivity', and to state when it is my own thoughts and feelings I am recording. I believe that recordings should be put to work. This is their value and purpose, the distinction between an onerous task and a practical work-aid.

What use are recordings?

By referring back to notes of previous meetings and individual clients' folders, and by a process of appraising and evaluating previous work, weekly objectives are set in team meetings. These meetings provide the opportunity for each worker to inform the team of the strategy for, and progress with, individual clients or groups using their recordings for reference. I began a system of using recordings as a basis for supervision during training, and have continued this practice. These provide the opportunity for me to analyse my interventions in some depth, with the help of my supervisor. I prefer to select a piece of work with which I am having some difficulty, evaluate it and plan future ways of working. This process can be uncomfortable, but is both challenging and thought-provoking.

Decisions taken at case conferences, reviews and planning meetings often have far-reaching effects for the client. Material from the client's folder assists me in making a contribution, and when possible I make brief notes to prepare myself in advance, especially if the client will not be attending in person. Several times I have heard other workers say, 'Oh, but I'm sure s/he would feel ...' and then go on to make an assumption about the wishes of the young person concerned. Getting beyond assumptions is important. I have learnt how an overall picture may emerge at such meetings from small pieces of recorded evidence. At one meeting, from seemingly unrelated and minor incidents recorded by individual workers, a picture of what appeared to be a case of child abuse emerged as people round the table made their individual contributions. The hypothesis was eventually borne out.

Individual clients' casenotes are also invaluable when writing a court report after an initial assessment period, or when a client has re-offended. From these notes, I am able to provide an account of changes in attitude and behaviour, tasks accomplished, responses to challenge, skills acquired or changed circumstances. It is also usual to record areas in which the client would seem to continue to experience some difficulty. Information of this type is particularly useful in the writing of a closing report when a client comes to the end of their time at the project.

In particular there are issues such as Steve's drug abuse (which he assures me is no longer a serious problem), his frequent lack of sleep and the fact that he rarely eats properly. Steve also seems to suffer from occasional bouts of depression. His unemployment situation is also significant. More than once, Steve had said to me that he still fears he might revert to his 'old ways' i.e. stealing, if he is consistently short of money.

The aim of the report is to inform the supervising officer of the client's progress on the scheme, setting out their strengths and achievements, but also detailing areas where there would still seem to be work to be done. In addition to the use of recordings for monitoring and evaluating routine work, the information could be used when examining the work of the project in a broader context, such as providing the basis for an annual report or as evidence to accompany an application for funding or equipment.

For the client, the running record provides visual evidence of personal development during their period of attachment. Changes in behaviour may be both positive or negative. Some young people find written records of their strengths and weaknesses as perceived by me as a worker difficult to accept; others enjoy and learn from looking back over their time at the project.

Andrew spent time looking at his file. He seemed surprised at the variety of things he had done in the time. Andrew reacted quite strongly when he realised that the strong racial prejudice he frequently displays had been recorded. Andrew did not contest the accuracy of the recording, but said that 'it didn't look too good' written down, and wondered why I had thought his attitude worth noting. We spent the remainder of his session discussing this.

Problems and issues in recording

My agency, like many others, has a policy of open access recording. The question for me is how the client will benefit from seeing their file, rather than whether or not they have a right to see it. In our project, access would be given to the running record, and any other reports written by ourselves. The keyworker, however, may ask for certain information to be withheld (subject to approval), on the grounds that it would be in the best interests of the client to do so. Judgments of this sort can be extremely difficult to make, and might seem to contradict the aim of open access. Conflict regarding content is less likely to arise because of the methods of working employed. The basis of our work is challenging attitudes and behaviour in a positive way to effect change. We do not aim to 'label' young people in the process. Consequently, we would be unlikely to record anything which we have not 'worked with' in some way with the client. However, counselling is still important in this respect prior to the client seeing the file, in the company of the worker. There is something fundamental about writing, changing a verbal 'of the moment' interaction between client and worker into a permanent form which could then be shared by many. A problem also arises when a recording is made of some information disclosed by a third party: this could be a parent, sibling or worker from another agency. This material is not covered by open access policy and may not be disclosed to the client without permission. This raises issues about how to record the information. Whichever way it is done, the worker is then in possession of information about the client of which the client may be unaware and which might in some way affect the working relationship.

A question about confidentiality follows. Should information freely given by a client and recorded by me as a worker then be passed on to the client's supervising officer? If I do not make him or her aware of any significant pieces of information, can we then effectively work in partnership to assist our mutual client? What happens is that clients are made aware from the outset that information given to individual workers within our own agency is in reality given to the agency as a whole, and that any significant information will in turn be passed to their supervising officer. Arrangements are not so easily defined for workers in other outside agencies.

The knowledge that certain information will be passed on may, of course, inhibit the client's working relationship with ourselves. There may be occasions when clients disclose information about offences for which they have not been caught. This puts the worker in the difficult position of having to decide whether or not to record the information. I would usually opt for noting the basic details, in order to do some further work with the young person. The question I would ask is why the client chose to give me the information and what they thought I would do with it? What did they expect to gain from telling me? As it stands, as I understand it, the information is hearsay and I am not legally bound to pass it on. The moral obligation, however, is a different issue. Fortunately, we have not yet had a case where the client has not, after having worked through the issue, decided to made an official disclosure. However, if a client made us aware of an offence they were planning to commit, we would then be legally bound to inform the police. As far as I am aware, there is no formal agency policy regarding this very difficult area of our work.

This leads to the question of what to choose to record. Events may only prove significant in hindsight. The idea of recording observable behaviour in an attempt at objectivity seems straightforward. In practice, I have found that this is not always so. Something reported by one person about another must carry some bias, however conscientious the writer is. This could be exacerbated by the knowledge that the client has access to the file. The issue of language is also raised in this context. Many of our clients have difficulty with reading. Should this knowledge then affect the way I record? How do I check out the client's understanding of what I have written, when their perspective must be different from my own, if for no other reason than because I am the worker and they the client? Certainly, comprehensive, verbatim records which the client might find it easier to identify with are simply not feasible because of time limitations. A process recording of one hour's counselling would take at least the same time to compile. Thus the interpretation of significant issues or events is left to me as worker. I know I do not always record as fully as I should because of lack of time.

I have already made clear what I consider to be the value of recording. The problem for me is the value put on them by others. I think a specific time should be set aside at the end of the day to record. This view is not universally shared. I once complained to a colleague about having difficulty keeping up with my recordings and was told 'That's how it should be.' A major part of our work is labelled 'crisis intervention'. This label seems to be used by some workers as permission not to record. If the intervention was truly in response to a crisis, should not recording it be equally critical? The question of value also arises when making recordings of work with clients for whom I am not keyworker: for example, during a colleague's absence. Do I record as thoroughly for those clients? I know how frustrating it can be to return from an absence to find that little of the work done has been written down, but recognize it is easier to be conscientious when I have 'control' of the work as keyworker.

The issue of enabling young people to participate in the decision-making has also arisen for me. As workers, we are seeking to encourage our clients to accept responsibility for their actions. A more effective way of working might be for clients to be fully involved in the process of recording, for them to recognize and record changes in their attitudes, behaviours and the acquisition of skills, with the worker assisting and facilitating the process. This might alleviate concerns about clients' access to recordings. The same might apply to court reports, with the young person being invited to write the report with the help of a worker. Clients are asked in court about their commitment to the scheme. Without such commitment there is little point in offering an alternative which is dependent on a high level of co-operation. Maybe a collaborative approach would be an effective beginning.

Conclusion

My aim in this chapter was to express thoughts and feelings, advantages and pitfalls, both practical and theoretical, resulting from my experience of keeping records. Two points have emerged for me from this exercise.

First, it has reaffirmed my belief in the use and value of recordings, and my acceptance that this attitude is not shared by all other workers. Despite my recognition of the importance of the task, I know that I am not always as conscientious as I would wish to be. Regular recording requires a high degree of self-discipline, but I know that if I want to increase my effectiveness as a worker, one sure way is to regularly record, analyse and learn from my everyday practice. This way of working does not seem to coincide with some people's image of a 'caring' professional. It is as if to 'care' the worker must demonstrate this through a casual, 'laid-back', slightly disorganized style. This philosophy does not rest easily with me. For me, caring is about giving the best possible service to the client, who after all is starting from a position of disadvantage. If recording assists me in becoming a better worker, then I am all for it. Certainly, I favour relaxed, informal methods to fulfil the primary task of my agency, providing I also continue to monitor and evaluate in order to respond appropriately to the changing needs and circumstances of the client/s. Good recording is a safeguard for both client and worker. This would seem to be emphasized in the current climate of accountability with the social worker carrying heavy and difficult caseloads requiring a high degree of professionalism.

Second, it seems to me that there is a danger in the work that I do of focusing entirely on the 'end-product', a reduction of re-offending rates, in order to justify the existence of such schemes. Surely some consideration should also be given to the process undergone by each client, and the changes that have occurred as a result. Maybe a client does re-offend, but the offence could be less serious than before, or a significantly longer time might have elapsed since the last offence. We are attempting to change behaviour patterns which have been established during a socialization process of many years. The changes are often very small, but significant nevertheless. Our evidence of this process is contained in the running record of each young person on the scheme.

Questions for consideration

1   What are the effects of recording being given such a low priority in most social work offices? How might it be given a higher priority?
2   Is it ethical to make recordings about your clients with which they disagree?
3   How can you balance out your own needs with those of your agency and your clients in deciding what and how to record?
4   Is there anyone who keeps records about you? What is the reason for this, and how are your interests safeguarded?
5   How might new technology and recent legislation regarding data protection affect recording in social work?

4

Counselling in a Social Services Area Office: The Practice behind the Theory

JEREMY WALKER

Counselling is something that many practitioners and students have an interest in. Post-qualifying courses in counselling are popular. However, social workers frequently see counselling as an activity which it is difficult, if not impossible, to undertake in their day-to-day work. Consequently some are to be found in a voluntary capacity working for counselling projects that cater for specific groups such as the bereaved, young people and families. They argue that it is only within such settings that counselling is properly valued. In busy area offices or child-care teams counselling is pushed aside by other roles and demands, by the need to deliver resources or undertake depersonalized bureaucratic tasks. Yet the belief persists for many social workers that counselling is the most desirable mode of intervention, it is the way they would like to work if only time and space allowed.

Jeremy Walker recognizes that many social workers, faced with seemingly unsurmountable problems, feel perpetually inadequate. He describes his own acknowledgment of the troubling feeling that he was offering a service that fell far short of what he thought it should be. In this chapter we are invited to share the author's analysis of the meaning of these constant feelings of failure, the contrast between what he thought he should achieve and how things often turned out.

Through confronting his feelings of powerlessness in the face of what seemed to be overwhelming demands upon his time and capacity to deliver help to clients, he has constructed a set of golden rules for himself about counselling.

This account provides an example of a different, perhaps more explicit, level of theory-making than in some of the other chapters. Nevertheless, as we described in Chapter 1, his golden rules are an explicit attempt to extract theory from practice – the practice behind the theory, as his title describes it – rather than to squeeze practice into theoretical frameworks. He emphasizes the necessity of individual workers making their own subjective journey as they attempt to work therapeutically. In offering his own story he provides some signposts by which readers may commence their own journeys.

Many will find this chapter extremely helpful in enabling them to gain perspective in their work. They will recognize the possibility of social workers trying to control clients, a danger which can arise through the good intentions of therapy. Others will disagree with this analysis, and particularly with Jeremy Walker's suggestion that social workers sometimes contribute to their own problems through unrealistic expectations of themselves and others. Whatever the initial reaction, readers will no doubt find themselves reflecting more deeply on just what their direct work with clients, whatever the setting, entails.

Readers will also be encouraged to think about the extent to which counselling can be combined with other social work roles; whether everyone can be helped through counselling; what kind of supervision is needed for counselling; and how we can guard against the dangers of imposing our own solutions on our clients. We can learn much from this honest and committed account.

* * *

Sitting at my desk between appointments, I asked a very experienced colleague if she did much counselling in her work. She replied, sounding slightly embarrassed: 'I don't know – if you mean talking to someone when their husband is becoming demented or about to go into Part III, or if they've had a bereavement, well yes. But if you mean having people in for a fixed time, that kind of thing, well I don't do any of that now.' I turned to another colleague who recently finished her qualifying course and asked her the same question. She said: 'No, not really – it's "do this", "do that", "phone that person", "get this sorted out". We're either processing paper or people towards an end we've long since lost sight of. At the same time, this thing called 'counselling' is gradually fading from view or seeming like an anachronistic relic from a golden age: or we're 'doing it', or think we're probably doing it, often automatically, *ad hoc* and on the run: on the telephone, when clients call in on spec, on home visits and so on. If we decide to have a go at something more structured, we may feel a bit sheepish or furtive, and that we need a special dispensation from the powers that be. Formal counselling is something that other people tend to do: colleagues in Child Guidance or family therapy clinics. We envy them because they have their own rooms and can hive off unpleasant statutory work, and do not have to spend all day ringing round the country for emergency placements for children.

Counselling is now formally enshrined in mainstream child-care law. The 1989 Children Act replaced the 'advice, guidance and assistance' of the 1980 Child Care Act with 'advice, guidance and counselling', which should be available to children in need living with their families. It is something that most of us employed in local authority social services departments want to do, at least for part of the time. Our own personal inclinations, and certainly our training, gear us up for this. For good or bad, it is a relatively high-status activity which is generally valued above, say, the provision of practical help or care. Ours is a rather low-status profession and we have to work in under-funded offices, often on main roads with traffic rumbling by. We know we have to be accessible to users or potential users, but this often leads to our feeling overwhelmed or exposed. As a group we suffer from recurrent bouts of Seligman's (1975) learned helplessness in the face of the random stimuli of demand. People come through the street door into reception for just about every reason imaginable: to use the lavatory because the public ones are closed; to use the phone to chase up a late giro; because they have mistaken us for the Department of Social Security; to leave their children because they are at their wits' end; or because they have to have somewhere to take their suffering.

Counselling is an oasis of order, calm, and therapeutic hope which beckons but which often turns out to be a mirage. In reality conditions tend to be characterized by disorganization which is reactive and anti-therapeutic. Supervision, instead of being a rigorous examination of direct work with clients, has a tendency to be defensive or collusive. That is to say, it is either concerned simply with ensuring that whatever needs to be done to ward off criticism from virtually any quarter is done, or (and perhaps as a counterweight to the first tendency) it is primarily directed towards providing social workers with a supportive, empathic response to help them survive in the hostile territory in which they operate.

This chapter is intended as a survival guide for social workers who, for good, sound reasons, want to provide counselling in their work but who feel they are struggling against the odds. My intention is not so much to lessen the odds, which I suppose would be an achievement, but to do away with the metaphor. Twelve years post-qualification experience, both as a genericist and mental health specialist in a social services area office, have made me aware of a number of cardinal rules governing most therapeutic work. The first of these is that many of the difficulties we encounter are actually of our own making. This is not a popular view because it is easier to attribute them to lack of support from our employers or to the client who is 'difficult', 'manipulative' or 'unmotivated'. Faulty assumptions, lack of clarity, sometimes a basic but understandable confusion about the proper nature of counselling or the therapeutic exchange all contribute to a sense of struggle against both the odds and the client, rather than an atmosphere of challenge or joint enterprise with the client. There are, of course, plenty of important and relevant issues that as social workers we need to concern ourselves with, such as lack of funding or resources; the demands of central and local government policy, and of new legislation; and so on. But we are morally and professionally obliged to ensure that in the time we spend with clients, while we may be baffled or unsure about whatever they might bring, we can at another remove achieve the poise and single-minded concentration that is essential for good therapeutic work.

What follows is simply what I have learnt from my own casework and observations in an inner London social work office. It is theory distilled from practice rather than practice knocked into shape to fit pre-existing theories which may feel congenial. The clients in question are probably fairly representative of users of local authority social work across the country. I owe much more to them than they do to me because in being open and true to themselves they have enabled me, rather late in the day, to edge my way towards being 'good-enough' in my direct work instead of just muddling through.

Most are women and lone parents; they tend to have material or financial problems, and to be disconnected from their families of origin. For those with children the most central or pressing issue is that of control. For women with younger children the fear or danger tends to be that in trying to establish control they may abuse them. Where there are older children, on the other hand, they have either evaded parental control almost entirely by truanting from school, staying out at night and drifting into prostitution or drug misuse or, in the case of boys, the absence of control and containment, and of gradual adaptive separation at an early stage, returns in the form of violence or threats against mother in adolescence. Most have had attention from professional helpers over many years, and some as a result have come to suffer from a kind of network-induced distress. This arises when clients are in contact with a number of professionals operating from different theoretical standpoints (or no acknowledged theoretical standpoint at all), who may be giving wholly conflicting advice. With each new contact, hopes for change may be raised initially but the same ground is gone over, perhaps in different ways. Quite quickly the client becomes disappointed or frustrated, and the behaviour or problem which attracted the attention of professionals originally may be amplified. This may draw more helpers into the system, and any attempt by clients to disentangle themselves from the network may attract yet more attention.

This is in fact a growing problem. Keyworkers in children's homes or mental health hostels, fieldworkers, health visitors, GPs, teachers in their pastoral work, psychologists, education social workers, priests and many others may all, at different times and levels, and in very different ways, be offering the same client counselling in one form or another. School nurses, too, see themselves as being 'vital ... in offering ongoing support and counselling' to children with emotional problems (*The Independent*, 8 August 1991). Counselling has cachet but takes place in camera; this is a dangerous combination and one we will return to later.

What all these clients have in common is that none would be considered suitable for conventional psychotherapy. Most have what psychiatry would describe as personality difficulties: many struggle with intense internal pressure which sometimes erupts into bizarre, impulsive or aggressive behaviour at times of increased external stress. One called this her 'depression' and, when passing through this phase, would come down to the office and be verbally and physically aggressive. She told me she saw the office as somewhere where she knew she could go and do this without repercussion or retaliation: 'I just come down to you lot and let you have it.' Two other clients, who had both been abandoned as very young girls, would (again at times of high stress) refuse to leave the office after a session. This behaviour would gradually draw more and more people into the arena, including the team manager, office manager, and eventually the police. Each would try in different ways to find out why the client was behaving like this although, in her confused and paralysed state, she could not possibly really know the reason for her behaviour. Leaving was simply impossible because, at a level beyond the reach of awareness, to be made to leave was to be abandoned.

A final characteristic which many of these clients shared was to come to the office with an apparent solution in mind: 'If I could be rehoused, I would not be so depressed, so angry inside;' 'If you could, instead of talking to me, come and tell my son not to hit me, to go to school;' 'If I had more adaptations done to the house, my disabled son would not be so hyperactive and at risk of injury.'

For a number of years after qualifying, my work with clients such as these might have seemed to an outsider a model of good, virtuous social work. I was tenacious and reliable; I offered them structure and empathy, and non-possessive warmth. I allowed ventilation and exploration of feelings. On the inside, however, I was in difficulties. I felt out of control and troubled. It would be easy to say I was picking up the projections of the client and that these were counter-transferential feelings which provided an insight into the inner world of the client. The following intrusive thoughts which repeatedly distracted me will probably be familiar to most social workers and show that the process is rather more complicated. They would occur in various permutations, but we can see that there are common themes.

- Am I doing this well enough?
- Am I out of my depth/not expert enough?
- Would another agency/person do this better?
- Will I get into trouble if I miss something?
- Am I getting through?
- If I could give this person practical help, would that be better?
- Will this person come back?
- I wish this person would go away
- I wish this problem would go away
- This seems hopeless/overwhelming
- I want this person to see things my way
- I am having intrusive/irrelevant thoughts

- I wish I did not have to do this
- I wish I could be at a meeting instead
- I am not getting through and it feels frustrating/horrible
- I want to get this over with

I have come to realize that these background ruminations are coloured by an immensely complicated network of relationships, perceptions and expectations, and in turn give information about them. They are funnelled through me and the client into the transaction or space between us. My relationships with my supervisor and agency, and even with colleagues in other disciplines; how I and the client see each other, and what we represent for each other; what the client and even society and the law, expect of me or my agency; all these, to different degrees and in different combinations, play their part in shaping what is an exchange between two ordinary people in an ordinary room, trying between them to make things better. At another remove, questions of race, culture, gender and language find their way through the medium or lens of the individual into this modest, faltering enterprise, and all these factors are finally distorted or refracted by the two personalities and pathologies involved.

I have been fortunate to have had three years of individual therapy and for four years to have used the family therapy model of live or group supervision through video or one-way screen. These have all helped me towards the combination of confidence and openness which is essential in all therapeutic work with clients. However, they are not available to everyone and were not enough on their own to help me make the transition from feeling lost to enjoying the journey to an unknown destination.

I have gradually become more willing to listen to, or acknowledge, the inner voice and outer currents described above, but came up against a difficulty or apparent paradox. The more I heeded them the more I felt mesmerized or paralysed by them. To be effective I knew I had to be aware, but in being aware I felt powerless. In listening too hard to wider rhythms I felt I was becoming deaf to the special nature of the individual transaction. Fear, or the impossibility of confronting this apparently insoluble paradox, led me to prefer simpler, neater activities, such as providing practical help or statutory work under child-care or mental health legislation.

With time, however, I have gradually come to my own conclusions which I think is probably the only way that any of us can become effective and confident in our work with clients. In a way this chapter is inherently contradictory. I make recommendations, the leading one of which is that it is only by working things out for ourselves that we can make progress in our counselling work with clients.

The first step is to look out for feelings that have their origin in a wish to be omnipotent. Many of the thoughts I have described above come from a belief that I could or should be brilliantly effective; the discomfort I was feeling came from the realization that this was not the case. I rather suspect that it was a desire to be omnipotent that attracted me and many others to social work in the first place, and it is probably occupationally quite normal. It is best, I think, not to resist thoughts of this kind because that tends to make them more intrusive and troublesome. It is better to be open and even good-humoured about them, and the proper arena for that is supervision. Unfortunately there are some endemic problems in supervision in social work in addition to the ones mentioned above. In the time immediately after qualification we are keen to show we know what we are doing, but we very quickly pass into the phase where we feel we should know what we are doing because we are experienced. This makes it very hard to be completely open about what we feel to be our shortcomings and about what is in any event a very difficult job.

The other main antidote to omnipotence is experience. There are again organizational difficulties because social workers tend to get promoted rather early out of direct work into management, and also tend not to stay working very long for the same local authority. There is nothing more salutary than meeting former clients, perhaps in the street, and discovering that they are going along in the same groove as years before and how far this differs from my original aspirations for them. In my view all clients should be followed up perhaps a year after contact with them finishes, so that information about them and their views about their contact with the department can be fed back into the system.

Golden rules, faulty assumptions

Consent, contract, common ground

Beginnings are absolutely crucial: in the first 1–3 meetings the tone and nature of all future work is likely to be set. Once a particular relationship between social worker and client is set in motion, attempts to change it in midstream to something more measured and therapeutic will be influenced or undermined by that initial relationship.

The nature of counselling, the method of working, the proposed length of contact, and the expectations that the social worker has of the client must be made explicit so that informed consent can be given. With a child this should involve both child and parent, even if the child is in care or in accommodation provided by the local authority or other agency. Careful thought must be given to whether there is common ground between social worker and client. The following questions have to be addressed: does the client accept the central premise of counselling, namely that talking together can produce change? What are the client's expectations of the department, of the social worker and of working together? How does the client use the department or office? One client, with a long history of paranoid schizophrenia, once told me that I was his friend. I handled this rather clumsily and he obviously felt rejected and that I was in some way terminating our relationship. He said he couldn't stop coming to the office 'because it's mother's milk, you see'.

Compliance should not be mistaken for consent: one should not underestimate the desire to please. I can think of a number of cases of my own and colleagues in which clients have gone along with individual or family therapy out of deference or obedience to figures in authority rather than a belief in the therapy itself. Casework of this kind may go on for months or years and be cited as evidence that progress is being made; or, just as likely, that the client is resistant and therefore contact must continue. I have adopted the practice of offering sessions over three or, more usually, six months, after which there is an enforced break and the client then has to decide whether to re-apply for further sessions.

The theory of opposites, and archetypal relationships

Jung's (1979, p. 425) observation that things tend easily to become their opposites is particularly relevant here. There is a very fine line between therapy and a form of tyranny in which the hidden and perhaps unconscious aim is to coerce the client into a particular course of action or way of seeing the world. Theories are tools for ordering information, not world views, which sooner or later the client has to come to share. Counselling should not be a means of imparting a view of how individuals or families function to the client. We should constantly refer to Jung's principle and ask ourselves if we are straying over the line.

There is a tendency also of all relationships to fall into an archetypal arrangement of dominant/dominated. This should again be carefully guarded against in all casework relationships, especially where care and counselling are provided under the same roof and even by the same people: for example, in children's homes and mental health hostels. In my view, in all therapeutic relationships, whether what is being provided is called counselling or psychotherapy, the client must at all times be truly free to leave: this is on both moral and therapeutic grounds (which may in fact come to the same thing).

Policing, processing, parenting

In social work there is particular danger of role confusion, and over-load for that matter. Therapy has to be carefully disentangled and set apart from other functions. Clients who are expecting us to be processing them through to other departments or resources can fall foul of our wish to be providing therapy. I recently visited a young man with a diagnosis of schizophrenia who wanted to leave home to move into a mental health hostel. This involved filling in an application form and providing a social history. I spent an hour or so with him, briefly gathering factual information first, and then enquiring about relationships at, how they affected him, his level of motivation and maturity, and so on. It was only after I left that I realized I had forgotten to explain to him in any way why it was necessary for me to be looking at these issues.

Similarly, the primary need may be for policing/protecting, through the Children Act or Mental Health Act, or for parental skills on the part of staff in children's homes or hostels. Our wish or urge to provide therapy, in its broadest sense, becomes intertwined with these functions which are weakened and distorted as a result. There are numerous child-care cases (Jasmine Beckford, Stephanie Fox and others) where this confusion has had fatal consequences. It can still surface at child protection case conferences where the main thrust may be therapeutic rather than protective. This is especially true if a parent is present, as increasingly happens. Instead of concentrating on assessment of risk, on what constitutes adequate parenting and on what ways of disciplining children are acceptable, conference members may compete with each other to be the 'good therapist', questioning and counselling the parent about his or her difficulties. Mistaking exploration of a problem for its management is easily done, but dangerous.

'There is no one who can't benefit from counselling'

We are critical of the way in which psychotherapy is generally highly selective, with strict criteria for assessing suitability for treatment, and tend to go to the other extreme. We think that if a problem is identified there must be an attempt to solve it, usually through counselling of some kind.

This is often justified with some observation such as 'it's a complicated family set-up', or 'there are interesting family dynamics', or even 'there's a lot going on'. There are particular events which tend to trigger our therapeutic interest, such as bereavement, separation, illness and so on. This is partly, it has to be said, because of our tendency to see causality in a linear, historical way and to overlook the subjective significance of events for the individual. One of the consequences of this is that it is easy to overlook small, discrete areas where counselling may be of real help.

To deny someone the opportunity for counselling can feel like depriving them of a basic right, and can expose one to criticism from other agencies. With some clients, who have come regularly and appeared to have faith in my ability to help them, I have convinced myself that I have been doing good work. Prolonged contact with them may reveal more and more events or dynamics which have persuaded me that it is essential for contact to continue. In retrospect, however, I can see that the therapeutic relationship was in fact a hollow one and that there was no movement or growth, first because there was no common ground: second, I made the mistake that so many of us do of failing to realize that uncovering is not the same thing as learning from.

I have seen colleagues gradually become tangled up with such clients whose relationship to therapy has an almost addictive quality. Far from getting relief from their contact with the department, their distress may intensify and become unmanageable. I believe these relationships often arise out of an urge to repeat earlier, unsatisfactory ones which are like fragments of experience that we all at times feel compelled to return to, like a smell captured in a bottle. In many cases the aim of work should be less rather than more. Weaning people away from therapeutic relationships which they cannot handle, or which it is the wrong time to embark on, may in itself be the most therapeutic thing we can offer.

Timing, as well as being selective, is important. Procedures should be flexible to take account of this. Some people should be seen quickly or immediately, to harness the impetus for change: for others, it is better if they are asked to take their time to think carefully about what it is they want and then re-apply.

Respect the problem as well as the person

We have to strive to become indifferent to the problem. This is not possible, of course, if we have a policing or parenting role. A problem can be, as Jung (1968, p. 31) put it, an island defence where a person can take refuge in a sea of greater troubles, so beating your child may be preferable to being overwhelmed by your child; allowing your son to push you around may be preferable to being assertive, which may bring certain penalties with it. This does not mean that we should not take the problem seriously, but that we must be neither for it nor against it. If we feel drawn to the objective problem or condition so that we want to root it out or confront it, or are even attracted to it, we have to think about its subjective meaning for us. We have to hear about a problem and understand it in such a way that the client feels we can grasp its significance or importance without wanting to knock it down or shut it away. As one client said to me recently: 'If I feel I want to kill myself, I want to be able to say that. It doesn't mean that I will but it also doesn't mean I'm not serious.'

Containment first, insight later

Effective counselling can only take place once trust has been established. This can only happen when feelings are first contained and then understood. The temptation always is to leapfrog these two stages and to try to enlighten the client about one's analysis of the problem. This is a mistake on two counts: first, most of the clients are not at the stage where they can be reflective and play around with ideas at this level. Second, without a proper formulation of the problem, of the client's relationship to it and feelings about it, the social worker is likely to be drawn into it, at which point all leverage and room for manoeuvre is lost.

The stage of containing and understanding may take a long time: in fact casework with a client may consist solely of this. Attempting to take work further or deeper may be felt as persecutory and may raise anxiety which binds the client into a therapeutic relationship which both parties find troubling and unsatisfactory. Having a formulation or working hypothesis which is constantly added to or changed helps to prevent work becoming stuck or repetitious.

There is almost nothing more frustrating for clients than to be going over the same ground, sometimes with different people, to no effect. This is a particular danger when there is a crowded network and professionals, perhaps believing they are helping clients to ventilate their feelings, fall into this trap. The result is that clients are caught in the cycle of hope–disappointment–despair. Some, who may have experienced this over several years, develop a pervasive sense of despair or of being wronged by professionals. As one client put it: 'digging around feels like a violation – people are taking something without giving anything in return'. What she needed was to feel understood and an explanation for the way she was feeling that fitted her way of seeing things. What she had been subjected to repeatedly was the archaeological approach in which professionals search for historical information in the hope that something of significance will turn up. This is the 'breakthrough mentality', which will probably be familiar to many of us and is very hard to shake off. You feel that if you can only ask enough of the right questions or make enough of the right interventions, you will eventually press the right button and relief and integration will follow.

Looking back over my work with a number of clients I can see I often committed this 'combination-lock' error, believing that if I could only turn the therapeutic dial in the right way, both I and the client would suddenly find ourselves in an ideal state, free from tension and struggle. This symptom of omnipotent thinking can often contaminate months or even years of contact with a client. The search for the 'right' interpretation will always jeopardize the finding of a good-enough interpretation.

When Jung wrote that: 'interpretations are only for those who don't understand', he meant that we can never fully understand the material or psychological worlds, and that interpretations are merely imperfect attempts to infer meaning or make connections. Sound therapeutic work requires there to be a truce between the wish to be omnipotent and the knowledge that we are not. If we can achieve this we can see our interventions as signposts to areas of meaning that we can jointly explore with our clients.

The benefits of intervention are almost always over-stated

In writing of 'primitive' peoples, Freud (1987, p. 67) noted their overestimation of the power of their wishes and mental acts, the 'omnipotence of thoughts', a belief in the thaumaturgic force of words and a technique for dealing with the external world – 'magic'. These tendencies live on in the form of therapeutic optimism. They are institutionalized because social work organizations have to justify their existence and keep arguing for more investment and resources. They are also collective, and this can often be seen cropping up in case conferences or network meetings where there is a kind of collusive idealism about what can be achieved with families. I have also gradually become aware of them in my own work with individuals and families. Every problem or form of distress that is presented to me seems to trigger in my mind's eye its ideal counterpart. I have a faint but powerful image of what, say, a relationship between a mother and her four-year-old son, whom she cannot control and feels she hates, should ideally be: or how the young schizophrenic man who was having difficulty separating from his parents would ideally be living. The client also, for a variety of reasons, invests me and other helpers with special, ideal powers.

The problem tends to sit in the middle, between me and the client, a constant source of frustration and a reminder of how far short of the ideal our work is falling. Both parties have to uncouple themselves from their ideals, rather than try to extinguish them in the way that we mistakenly try to extinguish problems. Issues and difficulties have to be unpicked in a spirit of joint endeavour, and from a platform of equal partnership. One of the reasons why some clients come with a ready-made solution, such as rehousing as mentioned above, or care for a wayward child, is that it is an attempt to deal with problems on the level of the ideal. The solution is a symbol for the ideal or the key which opens the way to the ideal. We can very easily be wrong-footed right at the outset by a client who approaches us in this way, and never manage to get to the point where realistic work can be done.

A ex-client recently left a message for me to telephone her. I had seen her on a number of occasions a year or so ago because she had been in despair about her fourteen-year-old son who had been out of school for over a year. I returned her call with some trepidation because I knew I had not shifted her problem and did not want to be reminded of this. She in fact wanted my advice about trying to get back to full-time work but at one point said: 'You know that business last year – I found it helped in a funny way. I realized you didn't have the answer and it was something I 'd have to sort out – and it's sort of better really.' This may often be the most that our involvement can achieve: that people can first live more easily with their problems and then find the strength to tackle them on their own.

Conclusion

Although it may sound rather prescriptive, I would like to end this chapter with a number of recommendations. We need to promote our counselling skills and make colleagues in other agencies aware that we see them as an important part of our job which we can carry out professionally. If we have a counselling role with a client, rather than a policing or providing one, we must have proper supervision on that aspect of our work. This need not be carried out by a line manager but, if there is no supervision of counselling, there should be no counselling. In my view counselling without supervision is never better than no counselling at all.

We should (where possible) provide counselling in a formal, structured but flexible way. If we do it in an informal *ad hoc* way, we should be able to point to strong grounds for doing so. Where a number of workers are involved the network, in conjunction with the client, should decide who will be counselling the client. This will free other members of the network to concentrate on other tasks. Any changes should be agreed by all concerned.

Counselling should be seen as one of many discrete social work functions: it is too important to be part of a jumble of services which we unload on clients.

Questions for consideration

1   How can we establish a spirit of joint enterprise with clients (the therapeutic alliance)? What are the best ways of doing this at the beginning of work with clients?
2   What are the different ways in which clients might use, or relate to, a helping agency?
3   Can the same person, or agency, combine different roles (policing, parenting, therapeutic, etc.)? If so, how and to what extent?
4   How can we assess whether someone might benefit from counselling?
5   (a) Should social workers who are offering counselling in their work be in therapy themselves?
    (b) When, if ever, is it legitimate to be providing counselling without supervision? Can this be done by peers?

References

Freud, S. (1987) *On Metapsychology*. Harmondsworth: Pelican.
Jung, C. G. (1968) *Archetypes of the Collective Unconscious*. London: Routledge & Kegan Paul.
Jung, C. G. (1979) *Psychological Types*. London: Routledge & Kegan Paul.
Seligman, M. (1975) *Helplessness: On Depression, Development and Death*. San Francisco: Freeman.

5

Policing

DEBORAH MARSHALL

A great deal of soul-searching is often encountered amongst students in the early stages of their training regarding the extent to which social workers are the 'soft cops of welfare'. The debates, although often predictable and repetitive, are too important to be lightly dismissed. Each year a number of students prematurely leave social work courses, citing as their prime reason a desire to avoid becoming part of a social control profession. Others complete the course and then use the qualification to gain entry into areas of work that they see as less tainted by 'authoritarianism'. Few practitioners openly embrace policing as either a description of their work or a style of practice they find attractive.

Deborah Marshall's own biography is not fundamentally at odds with this view. The chapter acknowledges her own unease with policing in the early years of her professional life, but she has been unable to leave debates about social control unresolved in the seminar room. Changing practices within both social work and probation, she argues, have given these debates new significance. Legislative changes have obliged her and other workers to find ways in which they can undertake a policing function within agencies that still retain a commitment to other forms of intervention. Looking back on her earlier career she now recognizes that some of her apparently more benign interventions were often unclear in their purpose and often disguised her authority.

At first sight the chapter might appear in sharp contrast to the preceding one. Policing and counselling are often seen as polar opposites, one rejected and one embraced, at least in theory, by social workers who see themselves as caring. These two chapters are in fact complementary; they show a similar process of facing up to the impossibility of the tasks which social workers frequently set for themselves. Both authors write of the unrealistic expectations they had of themselves, and sometimes of their clients. The solutions which they reach, although shaped within different settings, involve being honest with oneself and with clients about the nature of the work being undertaken. Clarity of roles is identified by both as crucial, and we are encouraged to reflect on possible confusions over roles within their own work.

Deborah Marshall's journey from general probation work through civil work to community service gives a variety of points at which different readers will identify with the issues she raises. For example, those in statutory settings other than probation will immediately understand her feelings regarding civil work. They will no doubt be prompted to ask themselves whether the Children Act has resolved the issues identified here.

Her section on community service contains particularly interesting examples of the relationships between theory and practice. One involves bringing together research findings regarding gender and race in the criminal justice system, and her own observations of the particular setting in which she found herself. She was able to use these different levels of analysis to effect changes in provision. This might seem a fairly traditional, if not altogether common, example of the use of social science knowledge in practice settings. The other example she uses is much less traditional: through reflecting on her cases and on her feelings about the work, she recognized that she was not feeling what she expected to feel. She was far less uncomfortable with policing than she expected. This willingness to be surprised is a significant dimension of the relationship between theory and practice which we are exploring in this book.

* * *

Ten years ago I would not have been able to relate the concept of 'policing' to my work as a probation officer, let alone write about it. In the current climate of 'punishment in the community' (PIC), national standards and breach procedures, 'policing' our clients is even higher on the political agenda, and consequently on the agenda of probation services across the country. The ensuing debates have encroached on even the most apolitical of practitioners, trained and nurtured as caseworkers on a diet of post-Freudian theories to locate problems within their clients. True, we were encouraged to draw on systems theory to understand the competing demands and pressures of other 'systems' on our clients' lives. The radical school of social work emphatically located policing as central to the statutory worker's role, but experience on placements, and later at work, continued to stress the casework model of working. This was essentially an individual pathology model with the worker as benign (though paternalistic) intervener. As students we rehearsed the care versus control debate carefully in our essays, but were offered few strategies to manage the conflict in practice. Inevitably, initial discomfort in my first job as probation officer in a field team with a generic caseload was quickly dispelled, or rather displaced under the twin pressures of a high caseload and agency constraints.

A welfare approach

Although probation work is primarily statutory work, little emphasis was placed on the inherent policing role a probation officer assumes in work with clients. The traditional dictum 'advise, assist and befriend' is redolent of the welfare approach. Things are changing, however, partly as an attempt to restrict the growth in the prison population. This centres around three main strategies:

(a) increasing the range of alternative disposals;
(b) changing the rules concerning release; and
(c) making it harder for courts to send people away.

Emphasis has increasingly been placed upon PIC for all but the most serious and dangerous offenders. As prisons overflow with petty recidivists, fine defaulters and remand prisoners so the probation service is looked to provide this. Therefore it has been pressured by the Home

Office to demonstrate that it can 'deliver the goods', i.e., that it can provide firm controls and challenging programmes which comply with national standards. Integral to national standards is a clear and consistent breach procedure, hitherto anathema to most probation officers.

Breach proceedings were rarely initiated in the past, even in the face of the most flagrant contravention of the conditions. For example, many clients simply did not report to see their probation officers as directed, a clear breach of one of the requirements of a probation order. Weeks, occasionally even months, could elapse between contacts without any action being taken. National standards for community service, recognized as a forerunner for national standards in other aspects of probation work, now allow for only three unacceptable failures to attend before breach proceedings must be instigated.

Yet I was not alone in finding my role intrinsically unsatisfactory. My work lacked purpose and direction. I comforted myself that I was not a member of the 'soft' police: I was a social worker in the criminal justice system. Although authority was implicit in my role I rarely exerted it, or so I thought. My clients had broken the law but I was a helper, not a punisher. Social enquiry reports for the courts mirrored this approach, tending to be detailed social documents chronicling an offender's progress (or, more usually, lack of progress) from birth to present day; they were rich in detail but weak in analysis, with often only a cursory mention of the offence or offences which necessitated the report in the first place. Although not intended to be pleas of mitigation, these reports frequently assumed the mantle of a social apology. Unsurprisingly, subsequent work with clients on statutory orders similarly avoided concentration on offending behaviour. Furthermore, there was little diversity of practice. The dominant model was an individual casework one, with little joint working, groupwork, or work with other agencies.

The tide has indeed turned, and many of the recent changes 'inflicted' on the probation service have been unwelcome and strenuously resisted. As white follows green paper, seemingly relentlessly, many (I count myself amongst them) see the probation service's social work base being insidiously undermined, although a rearguard action has been mounted from within. However, change often forces a reassessment and re-evaluation. What emerges is, I feel, a greater certainly of what is done well and of what needs changing. This is beginning to happen in the probation service, and has certainly occurred within my own work.

I have consciously chosen to locate my work within the broader framework of changes in the probation service, because they are by necessity interrelated. I hoped the reader will gain something from the dilemma I have wrestled with over the years because, with critical hindsight, I see that my work has benefited from enforced change.

To return to my first job as a generic probation officer: after three years of battling with individual problems and individual solutions, I was weighed down by the recognition that most of my clients were poor, bored and unemployed, and furthermore I could do very little to improve their lot. When discussing this with a friend or colleague I was often reminded of the colloquial term for this disillusion: the 'pissing in the wind' syndrome. If I am honest, I attempted to resolve the discomfort bred of my middle-class insight by adopting an attitude of collusive indignation. My clients became victims of an unjust system, their offending an inevitable consequence of their disadvantage. I could with skill and/or good fortune 'get them off' by persuading the courts to make probation orders. And it was a let-off. I constructed elaborate justifications for their often continued offending. It was invariably my failure, or anyone's failure but my clients. Naturally with this approach, I did not see my role as in any sense 'policing' my clients. After three years, however, I was disillusioned, worn down and dissatisfied. My clients liked me, and this was gratifying, but I was becoming increasingly uncomfortable in my statutory role as I aligned myself more and more with my clients. Had I but known it, I was suffering from cognitive dissonance (a mismatch between ideas/attitudes and behaviour). Excess cognitive dissonance is said to motivate change: it certainly motivated me. Again, with hindsight, it is easy to see why I chose a move to a probation team that allowed me to specialize in civil work.

Being a good guy

As a court welfare officer I believed I had resolved the dissonance in a healthy way. Now I was the 'good guy', both officially and with my clients. There was also the added attraction of status within the court. Unlike criminal reports, welfare reports are often crucially important in the final decision. Welfare officers, I would argue, have far more power than probation officers. The burden often weighs heavily on them, and civil work is consequently not a popular area of work for probation officers. For me it offered a convenient if lonely way out of my discomfort, for I found myself working in increasing isolation in my team, my colleagues being more than happy to pass the work my way with deep

sighs of gratitude and incredulity at my masochistic folly. It seemed to
be folly for, despite status in the courts, little status accrued to civil work
in the probation service.

Civil work offered me the chance to engage in a discrete piece of
challenging work with a clear focus. The purpose of my involvement
was to represent the best interests of the child(ren). Work was therefore
task-centred and usually short term, but above all it had a clear purpose.
For me there was satisfaction in being able to wield influence in tangible
and significant ways, which I felt to be in marked contrast to my criminal work. I also believed myself to be a benign representative of the
court: the one human figure in an alienating and frightening process for
those caught up in the battles over access or custody. Here I hope I do
not paint too naive a picture of the crusading welfare officer. I do still
feel my work was satisfying and worthwhile, but I also feel I now have a
greater understanding of the inherent power of the role, which at the
time I never fully acknowledged. I recognized even then the potential
power of my welfare reports, but I believed my intervention to be essentially benign. As in my first job, the exercise of statutory power became
disguised in a welfare cloak which conveniently masked the imbalance
of power between worker and 'coerced' client. Probation clients are
rarely voluntary clients. Welfare clients are not under the same statutory
obligations, but are fully aware of the implications of non-compliance,
which are far more serious in nature because of their children are
involved and the stakes are therefore higher.

Encounters between welfare officer and parent can assume an air of
theatricality: the parent is anxious to stage-manage the right image,
while the welfare officer is eager to downplay the power and overplay
the understanding and empathy. It is acutely difficult to discuss a person's most intimate history at a time of personal crisis for them, while
maintaining the appropriate distance necessary for objectivity. The dangers of collusion and partisanship are ever present. Because emotions
are usually heightened, it is difficult not to be drawn in. In fact, the
process almost encourages this. It is usual to conclude a welfare report
with a recommendation, which often amounts to taking one side against
the other. Having fallen into the trap myself I have learnt the painful
lesson that power can only be dealt with once its presence is honestly
acknowledged. The welfare report often became for me the vehicle to
disguise the power that frequently was not honestly dealt with in my
interactions with parents. The adversarial court process further shielded
me from the consequences of this power by placing the final decision in

other people's hands, thus absolving me of final responsibility. Again, it
is only really within hindsight that I have understood this process, which
has underlined for me the necessity of good supervision. This was not
readily available to me, since my supervising officers lacked experience
of civil work: there were then in my probation area a number of newly
appointed senior probation officers who had in common their skilful
avoidance of civil work. This problem has since been overcome by the
establishment of civil units, overseen by senior probation officers with
an interest and skills in this area. There is now the opportunity for good
support and joint working, which I feel would have helped me deal
more effectively with these issues and improved my practice.

Despite the issues I have raised, I found civil work at the time a challenging though largely comfortable area of work because of the match
between my beliefs and the role assumed. The policing aspect of the
work was, as I have said, laundered and therefore more palatable. I con-
templated my next move into community service with some foreboding.

Facing up to policing

For a mixture of personal and strategic reasons I found myself in a tradi-
tionally unpopular post: unpopular, that is, with those probation officers
with whom I felt an affinity. It is perhaps a peculiarity of probation work
that probation officers are actively encouraged to change jobs after
about three years. The tenure of specialist posts is normally a maximum
of five years. Community service was, and probably still is, seen as the
controlling arm of the service with its emphasis on punishment rather
than rehabilitation. Furthermore, I joined this section at a time when
national standards were being introduced. This was an attempt by the
Home Office to impose a stricter, more consistent, regime nationwide,
as inspections had revealed unacceptable divergencies in practice and,
more importantly, discrimination against women, black and disabled
clients. Bearing in mind that community service is a high tariff disposal
and therefore usually imposed as an alternative to a custodial sentence,
discrimination leads to earlier entry into the prison system. In the case
of women and black clients, research confirms this to be so. A typical
female criminal career might be conditional discharge → probation
order → probation order → prison, missing out community service and
probation-run day centres which are normally regarded as alternatives to
custody (Hudson, 1987). There are no female attendance centres and

courts are loath to fine women who are already in poverty, and this is a major causal factor in their offending (Carlen, 1988). Community service and day centres are often seen by the courts, and also by some probation officers, as male sentences (Dominelli, 1984). My own experience in community service confirmed this latter point. However, it was possible to increase the number of women on community service by developing more flexible schemes that could therefore accommodate women with domestic responsibilities. Provision to pay child-minding fees was also sought from the probation committee but, perhaps most importantly, it was necessary to educate colleagues and the courts that community service was available for women at risk of custody.

There is a wealth of evidence to confirm discrimination against black people in the criminal justice system. Afro-Caribbeans in particular have a shorter tariff and are going to prison earlier in their criminal careers, tending to miss out fines and conditional discharges and, in the case of males, probation as well (Hudson, 1989).

Community service was to be a personal as well as a professional test for me. I was uncomfortable with the discernible shift in emphasis in probation work from care of control. Personally, I had striven to avoid an overly 'policing' role. My new role forced me to face both the professional and personal dilemmas head on. The results were a great surprise to me. Far from feeling constrained, I felt liberated in my new role. There was no hidden agenda because I was, and was perceived by others as, exercising statutory power. I felt freed to concentrate on using my social work skills to improve the quality and range of placements, and to ensure equal access for all client groups. It was particularly satisfying to me that, during my time at community service, by adopting the methods described above, there was a steady rise in the number of women on community service orders.

The introduction of national standards did initially result in more clients being taken back to court in breach of one or more requirements of their community service order, usually for failing to work as directed, which amounts to not turning up on the agreed day to work. Three such *unacceptable* failures constitute a breach of the order. However, there is some discretion around what constitutes an acceptable or unacceptable absence. The original guidelines were prescriptive on this point, but were watered down considerably in the final version to the extent that practice changed very little. Initially, there were more breaches, but after a few months into the new standards the breach rate levelled off. However, when breach became inevitable I found myself in the new role of prosecutor when presenting the facts of the breach before the court, and then would wear my other hat as probation officer in recommending a particular course of action. Invariably the recommendation would be to allow the client a second chance to complete his or her community service order. An adjournment was usually sought to test out the client's motivation, and a subsequently good attendance and performance record could be used to mitigate the level of fine that had to be imposed for the breach.

John's case is a good illustration of this process. He was offered numerous chances to complete his community service before breach proceedings had to be instigated. By the time his case got to court he had had enough and did not want a second chance to complete the remaining hours. This would have left the court with no alternative but to revoke the order and resentence him for the original offence, possibly placing him at risk of a prison sentence. John's solicitor prevailed upon him to give it another go but, given his reluctance, I asked for an adjournment to test out his motivation. The court issued the usual warning about the consequences of non-compliance. Both I and John's solicitor followed this up in a more conciliatory manner. As a result, John worked exceptionally well over the following four weeks before he returned to court, and his good work performance was rewarded by a nominal fine.

I expected problems between myself and the clients I had to breach. The threat of breach was scarcely wielded in my previous work, let alone carried out, and I always viewed it in a negative, destructive light as something that would destroy any prospect of building a therapeutic relationship. Here was an apparent paradox. It was possible to care within a controlling framework. There was a refreshing honesty in my dealings with clients. The rules of the game were made explicit at the outset. Indeed, many clients commented that they preferred community service to other more therapeutic sentences (for instance, a probation order with a condition of day centre attendance which is an equivalent sentence on the tariff). Completion of a stated number of hours of unpaid work was a tangible goal, with clear responsibilities. The instigation of breach proceedings followed a standard system of warning letters. At each point in the process it was possible to intervene and cancel warnings after interviewing the client and establishing their reason for absence. It was surprising how little resentment often accompanied these interviews. Even when breach proceedings became inevitable, most clients accepted the decision, particularly when they knew they would have a chance to try again and thus redeem the situation. Mutual candour characterized these exchanges, which I found surprisingly refreshing.

> *Me*: I'm afraid there is no alternative but to breach you. You have had three unacceptable absences and I told you at the beginning what the rules are.
>
> *Client*: Yes, I know. I've used up my three chances, but it's okay because I know I'll be able to finish the hours after I've been to court.

Because I felt confident that I had treated the client fairly, I felt comfortable in exercising authority. The challenge for me became getting as many clients through their orders as possible, and in fact under the rules of national standards more orders were completed, even though more breaches occurred.

Brian was a typical example. He was unpopular amongst the supervisors because he resented working for nothing. In fact he had never worked since leaving school and found it hard to conform to a work routine with set hours. In addition he had a chronic drink problem which meant he missed a number of days due to hangovers, and eventually breach proceedings had to be instigated. Like most people he was offered a second chance to complete the outstanding hours, although Brian had to be cajoled into accepting this chance. It took my colleague and myself a lot of time to work through Brian's anger and resentment about the controls and responsibility being placed on him. He eventually came to see that our control or policing of him was set in an overall context of care, and a desire to see him successfully complete the task set by the court.

Brian was placed with a sympathetic supervisor who took him under his wing and who viewed him as something of a challenge. His placement had previously been discussed in our weekly team meeting with the supervisors, when it was agreed with whom Brian would be placed. Thereafter, time had to be spent with the supervisor discussing potential problems and their resolution. Little paperwork was involved other than recording agreements, but several hours of negotiations took place between the various people involved. The project Brian was placed on was physically demanding (building a ramp for an old peoples' home) and required a range of building and labouring skills. Brian was able to see the project through from start to finish. Eventually he volunteered to work more days than required. By the time the breach was dealt with at court I was able to supply an excellent report which resulted in a nominal fine. Brian's probation officer commented that it was the first thing Brian had achieved in his adult life.

Although the primary goal of community service is not rehabilitation, by increasing the diversity of work placements and by offering clients as much choice as possible the outcome is often rehabilitative. The lives of many probation clients are characterized by failure and under-achievement. I was able to see first hand that for many of them community service was something they could achieve but, more importantly, it provided opportunities for them to give in ways that were clearly meaningful to them and unavailable elsewhere.

Tracey was resentful at having to do community service. Working for no money was anathema to her, even though she narrowly avoided a prison sentence. She was also clearly suspicious of probation officers and professional carers. Because of child-care commitments she could not work a standard day and had to be placed in an agency near her home where more flexible hours could be worked. The agency was a local authority old peoples' home. Tracey said she did not like old people and declined to work on the care side, so she was attached to the domestic staff. Her attendance was initially poor and she had to be warned. Eventually, however, she settled down and completed the order, earning praise for her good work and caring attitude towards residents, even though she was not attached to the care staff. This good report influenced the outcome of a subsequent court appearance when a further community service order was made. This time Tracey volunteered to work with the residents. She proved invaluable and totally reliable, so that when she had completed her community service she was employed on an occasional basis to cover staff absences. She is now a permanent member of the staff and earns enough money not to have to claim income support. Tracey was someone who benefited from (or at least responded to) a controlling structure, with a task-centred focus. This structure enabled her to be able to give and care for others in ways that were not previously available to her.

Conclusion

I have tried to convey some of the dilemmas and tensions that I have experienced during more than a decade in probation work. It is a deliberately personal account, which nevertheless I hope raises more general issues concerning the use or abuse of statutory power.

The majority of statutory work involves 'policing' clients in various ways, some of which are more overt than others. My professional development has run in tandem with significant changes in the probation service nationally. The official rhetoric has shifted from care to control, with a greater emphasis on 'policing' our clients. Autonomy has given way to accountability. Greater public scrutiny forced me to analyse my own work, and this had paradoxical results. Initially, in a climate sympathetic to the probation officer's caring role, I found my 'policing' role uncomfortable. It did not fit comfortably with my social work training or my own attitudes or beliefs. I therefore disowned this role to a large extent and, since publicly I was not required to exert my statutory authority, I was able to push the issue to the back of my mind. But since I wasn't 'policing' my clients the focus of my work was often unclear and ultimately unsatisfactory. I was able to engage with my clients and undertake 'social work' with them, but this was not related to an overall purpose or aim within the probation service or my own view of my work. I struggled to understand the purpose of my work. Civil work provided the clear focus I felt I had previously lacked. However, the exercise of authority, a significant aspect of the court welfare officer's role, became disguised in welfare issues. A dishonest interaction frequently developed due to my own inability to acknowledge the power inherent in my role. I fell prey to collusion and partiality. As court welfare officer I controlled covertly under the guise of caring.

In community service the control inherent in my role was explicit and therefore I was forced to acknowledge it openly. Any initial discomfort I experienced was quickly dispelled. My interactions with clients were refreshingly honest. There were mutual benefits. They seemed to appreciate knowing exactly what was expected of them and the consequences of non-compliance. I felt totally comfortable exercising my authority in this clear and explicit way. I was not pretending to be anything else; there was no hidden agenda.

The lessons I have learnt from ten years' practice may seem simple, even basic to a new practitioner or someone currently training. Nevertheless, I suspect everyone who works in a statutory agency must wrestle with the use of their statutory power to achieve a personal position that can be reconciled with their agency's requirements but, more importantly, which can form the basis of an honest interaction with their clients. To pretend that power does not exist may seem attractive, but is ultimately untenable and profoundly dishonest to both yourself and your client. If the reality of the relationship is spelt out at the outset, allowing your client to know both the rules of the game and the consequences if they are broken, the foundations are laid for a more effective relationship. It is not an equal relationship, but a professional relationship that affords the client the rights that she or he should expect.

The exercise of statutory power, whether in a more therapeutic role or an overtly 'policing' one, need not be a negative experience for either client or worker. It is possible to care in a controlling environment. It is perhaps still easier to control in an apparently caring environment. But professional integrity can be sacrificed on the altar of an easy conscience; proper respect for one's client will, however, be the ultimate sacrifice. Honesty is, after all, the best policy.

Questions for consideration

1   In what circumstances should probation officers recommend a custodial sentence?
2   Can middle-class professionals ever really understand the social and economic pressures that lead poor clients into offending? Have they any right to sit in judgment on their behaviour?
3   Should work with the elderly and disabled be used as a form of punishment?
4   How do you see the policing role fitting in with other social work roles?
5   To what extent is it likely that the Children Act will resolve the issues regarding civil work raised in this chapter?

References

Carlen, P. (1988) *Women, Crime and Poverty*. Milton Keynes: Open University Press.

Dominelli, L. (1984) 'Differential justice: domestic labour, community service and female offenders', *Probation Journal* (3), 100–3.

Hudson, B. (1987) *Justice through Punishment: A Critique of the 'Justice' Model of Corrections*. Basingstoke: Macmillan.

Hudson, B. (1989) 'Discrimination and disparity: the influence of race on sentencing' *New Community*, October.

6

Private Living in a Public Place

DEBORAH MANN

This account of life in a residential setting shows that it is both similar to, and different from, work in other arenas. Residential work has always been something of a cinderella service. Few enrol on courses in order to embark on a career in this sector. Low status, shiftwork and the difficulties of working in close proximity to clients all contribute to its unpopularity. Excessive staff turn-over and low morale have long been problems. This unpopularity is reflected in the relative absence of academic interest in this area of practice. Residential work is remarkably under-researched and marginalized within most training courses. Both staff and students commonly exhibit an absence of curiosity about the experience of residential life.

Residential work is affected, to a much greater extent than many field and community work settings, by a relative absence of social and physical boundaries which can protect the privacy of both clients and workers. On the other hand, questions about appropriate boundaries between private life and working life are important for all workers. Rather than simply seeing residential work as fundamentally different in this respect, it merely gives a sharper focus to the issues involved.

Other workers will, for example, have had to resolve the dilemmas arising from clients who contact them at home. These problems may be especially acute in small communities. This can be of great significance, for example, where workers and clients live in minority ethnic communities. In such situations clients will often know workers personally rather than simply in their official capacity. The relative absence of appropriate services from other agencies can intensify the feelings of workers that only they can help, even though it means sacrificing their time off. We can all benefit from identifying the various ways in which our private and working lives interact with each other.

As well as being applicable to all kinds of settings, Deborah Mann's account reveals many of the special complexities that flow from 'living on the job'. As this contribution shows, living in the public arena, and sharing the daily life of clients, presents workers with many challenges. It also offers unique opportunities. Workers cannot avoid controlling and managing the behaviour of their clients, or the requirement to balance the needs of the individual client with those of the community in which they and the worker live. Few social workers in other settings are obliged to do this, although it is a dimension that others might usefully reflect upon. Issues such as the place of friendship, when and where to intervene and the impact of an individual's behaviour on significant others are, after all, common to all aspects of social work. In residential work these questions take on a much more concrete shape, however, in the form of questions about hygiene, noise and clients' property.

One particular question which Deborah Mann's case studies raise is that of whether and how information about clients should be passed between different agencies. Like the discussion about confidentiality in Patsy Little's chapter on recording, this cannot be comfortably resolved by once-and-for-all technical, or even ethical, rules. Policies and practices regarding this question need to be worked through, taking account of ethical, legal, organizational and professional considerations. What is particularly important for workers is the work they need to do for themselves in clarifying their roles. Deborah Mann's honest description of how she moved from relative naivety, in an area of work which was unfamiliar to her and to her agency, to greater clarity, raises many stimulating questions.

* * *

Residential work is different from other forms of employment because, whichever setting it happens to be in, it means coping with the daily mundaneness and the stresses and strains that accompany the lives of everyone who shares that particular environment. The phrase 'residential home' conjures up various stereotyped images: pictures of incapacitated elderly people who need constant attention and assistance in everything they do; or of unruly youngsters who become institutionalized in the attempt to change their behaviour patterns into more socially acceptable forms. These, perhaps, are two of the commonest images. Homelessness, however, as media coverage testifies, is a growing problem, and hostels such as mine are seen as a viable alternative to the hated bed-and-breakfast accommodation which many councils have to resort to using.

The unit where I work is one of eight set up by the Housing Department of the local council, as part of its attempt to cope with the homelessness problem in the area. Any major change in policy affecting the units has to be discussed and passed by the Council's Housing Committee. The hostel is set on the outskirts of an old Essex town, which in itself can cause a few problems for some of the residents who have to travel into the town regularly to 'sign on' or visit one of the council offices. It is no fun struggling on and off a 'one-man' operated bus with a baby and toddler, or having to walk both ways in the freezing cold if you have not got enough money for the fare. The hostel, converted from a large guest house, has eighteen rooms of various sizes ranging from a tiny single room, which may be occupied by a mother and newborn baby for several months, to the largest one which might be used to accommodate a family. Downstairs there is a large communal kitchen and community room with a couple of easy chairs, while upstairs there are two smaller shared kitchens. Showers, bathrooms and toilets are located between the rooms and are shared facilities. The warden's accommodation, in the form of a two-bedroom self-contained flat, is located towards the rear of the house but encompassed in the main body of the building. At the back of the hostel there is a laundry and play area, and beyond this the car park. Originally there was a good-sized garden too, where the children were able to play and residents could sit out on the grass in good weather. However, this has now been completely obliterated and further accommodation, in the form of half-a-dozen mobile homes, has been sited for other homeless families.

The staffing consists of two wardens, myself and a non-residential deputy. There is also a cleaner who comes in each weekday to service the communal areas. As wardens we work a split duty of mornings and late afternoons with an 'on-call' night arrangement. Although officially our working hours do not overlap at any time, we invariably spend an hour or so each week discussing any problems we might have encountered and updating each other. We, in turn, report to the senior homelessness officer at our monthly wardens' meetings. This usually takes the form of an open discussion about individual or collective problems within the homeless units, and it is the only time specifically allocated for voicing grievances or airing views. We have no structured supervisory sessions and have to make appointments to discuss our individual needs or problems with the senior officer. One of the difficulties can be in establishing practical working relationships with the residents. At times it can be a challenge in itself to maintain contact with some individuals or families during duty hours. In contrast others seem to be constantly knocking at the flat door with one minor problem after another. In these circumstances getting the balance right is of the utmost importance, but it can be difficult to judge where to draw that invisible line. Being aware of each individual's right to privacy has to work both ways and, while some people seem to shun even the most basic amount of contact, others will deem it their right to speak to the warden at any time of the day or night. These are obviously two very diverse examples which may be encountered but it is worth noting that they do exist.

To 'provide support and assistance' as stated in my job accountability statement can cover so many eventualities that each individual case or incident has to be considered on its own merit, and I shall be exploring some examples later in the chapter. As wardens we receive very little background information on our residents unless, perhaps, they are termed 'vulnerable'; but, even in this situation, only limited details will be given. This can work in an advantageous way as it means that all newcomers should receive exactly the same treatment. It soon comes to light if someone does have a problem and details will emerge bit by bit as the resident chooses to open up or, if necessary, enquiries can be made to the Housing Department. From time to time this system can cause frustration on either side, when an individual's behaviour becomes unacceptable and there appears to be no obvious reason. On the whole I believe that it is important, initially, to accept the person with an open mind and without allowing feelings or actions to be influenced by past problems. However, to start with I think it will be of value to look at the more mundane aspects of the job and the day-to-day duties that are involved.

The daily round

A typical working day begins at 8.30 a.m. with a check around the building to make sure that everything is in order and, if the postman is early, the emptying of the post box and the delivery of the letters to the residents. If the post has not arrived there is usually someone hovering around the office soon afterwards enquiring about their mail and that all-important letter. For someone with no job or little contact with the outside world, receiving letters can be a way of validating their existence, or indeed providing the monetary resources for their actual living. It can be hard, though, to appreciate this when you feel constantly harassed by the same person whose only interest seems to lie in the contents of the post box. Other typical duties involve the collection of rent, electricity and other monies.

Obviously, cleanliness and hygiene are a very important factor in an establishment such as this, and as mentioned earlier we have been assigned the services of a cleaner who works each weekday for a couple of hours to help provide the necessary level of cleanliness. Unfortunately some of the residents seem to use this as an excuse not to do any cleaning themselves, and it is a constant struggle to try to establish responsibility for the cleaning of the ovens in particular. Although each room is allocated a small fridge in the kitchen area (for security reasons these are located in locked cupboards), all other facilities in the kitchens have to be shared with at least one other person, and cookers seem to bring out the worst in some people. Different standards of cleanliness probably cause one of the commonest complaints, and we are still trying to work out a foolproof formula to combat the hostilities between residents that seem to occur in connection with the tidiness of the kitchens.

Another of the everyday problems that arises from living in this type of establishment is the constant awareness of other peoples' noise. While a certain amount of tolerance has to be encouraged it can be very frustrating if you are trying to get your young child to sleep when the people above or below you are either having an argument or playing their music just a little too loud. It is inevitable that tempers are raised and arguments subsequently ensue when a family is having to live in one room for a matter of months, especially when they are unable to be given a likely date for moving on to something more suitable. Most people, once requested to be a little more thoughtful towards those around them, will do their best to comply; but it only takes one person whose attitude is, 'the more awkward I become the more likely I am to be given a place of my own', for the whole place to become fraught with tension. Unfortunately this view is sometimes correct, because if someone's behaviour is deemed intolerable by us as wardens, then we would invariably request that they be removed from the hostel. Needless to say this action is seen as a last resort and is not always viewed in the same light by the housing officials who do not have to live under the same roof as the awkward person. On one or two occasions action has been taken to avoid potentially explosive situations, and the 'offending' parties may be seen to jump the queue.

Another source of bad feeling can come from a spate of petty theft. It is always distasteful to have to warn people to be aware that not everyone has the same views when it comes to property, and even worse when something has gone missing and practically everyone is under suspicion. Initially when residents arrive they are noticeably careful with their belongings, but after a few weeks small items can start to be left lying around and may disappear into someone else's room, intentionally or not. Food is something else that has been known to go missing; perhaps the Sunday roast that was left on the side while you went to the loo is nowhere to be seen on your return, and no matter how hungry the other person may have been, it is no consolation to you when your taste buds were anticipating that nice succulent chicken. (Apologies to any vegetarians reading this.)

Security can seem at times an impossible part of the job. It is not unusual to find the front door ajar even though it has a large notice attached to it informing everyone that under no circumstances should this be the case. Not only can property go missing, but vulnerable residents may be at risk from ex-partners or so-called 'friends' who wish to confront them. Originally, too, the back door had an inadequate locking system, so it was impossible to ensure that only welcome guests and residents were present in the building. At the end of the day a security check is carried out by whoever is on duty; this usually takes place at 10.30 p.m. and will also entail making sure that all the ovens are turned off, any potential fire risk in the communal areas has been eliminated and that all visitors have left the building. It is not possible to be 100 per cent certain that every eventuality has been thought of or accounted for, but knowing the state of the building at that particular time is a useful reference point if anything untoward should happen later in the night.

Being in charge of a hostel means having responsibility not only for the residents but also for the building itself. Blocked drains, ill-fitting fire doors, lack of hot water or problems with the heating system; the list of maintenance jobs could go on and on. These are in addition to the 'one-off' incidents, such as dealing with a swarm of bees or trying to organize the fumigation of a room to counteract the near hysteria of some of the residents after the discovery of an individual's attack of scabies. In theory it should be relatively straightforward to phone the council repairs section and have each job noted and seen to. This is not always the case as jobs are categorized and, unless they are recorded as urgent, weeks or maybe months may transpire before they appear on someone's worksheet for the day. So not only is it important to be aware of the areas where problems are likely to occur, but it is also necessary to make periodic checks on the outstanding jobs to make sure that they have not been completely forgotten or become a hazard in the meantime.

It is inevitable with such a wide variety of responsibilities – inclusive of both people and place – that predicting a day's work is impossible. Occasionally some days may be so quiet they could even be termed boring, but at the other extreme there are times when the nights, as well as days, are filled with ongoing disturbances and the whole place seems beset with problems; certainly no two days are alike!

Rules for living

Looking back, it is somewhat disconcerting to note how my attitude and approach to the job has changed over the months. I started off with much enthusiasm and perhaps some naivety about the type of work that could be accomplished within the boundaries of the job. I imagined that a 'community spirit' could be achieved by regular meetings of all the residents, and envisaged babies and toddlers enjoying supervised play in the carpeted area adjacent to the laundry. Neither of these two examples has actually been achieved by any direct intervention from me, as I have learnt that it is the prerogative of the residents themselves to mix and converse with each other when and where they choose and not something that can be forced upon them. It has been necessary from time to time, however, to restrict the use of facilities to ensure the smooth running of the establishment.

One example of this can be recalled as a direct result of some residents taking advantage of the lack of rules and regulations associated with the life of the house. Initially neither myself nor the deputy warden had had any direct experience of working in a residential setting. The type of unit that had been set up by the council was, in fact, the first of its kind in the area; consequently there were very few guidelines to assist us in the running of the place, and we had very few rules and regulations. During the first few weeks the noise and activity within the house seemed to be ceaseless between the hours of 6 a.m. and midnight, and because several of the residents did not work and were therefore late risers it could often continue into the early hours of the morning. We realized that something would have to be done to combat this as, hardly surprisingly, it was giving rise to numerous complaints. It seemed ineffective just to ask the people concerned to be more considerate. Although they would comply for a day or two their pattern of living had been set and habits appeared too hard to break. We decided that to maintain a balanced environment it would be necessary to introduce certain limitations. These took the form of restricting the use of the communal areas after specific times. Obviously people could still use the kitchens to make a drink or snack, but they were asked not to socialize in these areas after a given time; likewise a curfew hour was set for guests to leave the building. The enforcement of such regulations was initially quite hard but, as the first residents moved on and new ones took their place, the acknowledgment that there was a genuine need for 'rules' became that much more acceptable.

At first it had almost felt that we were seen to be imposing our will on the residents, as they were given no real choice in the matter. If the behaviour patterns had been different it probably would not have been thought necessary to introduce restraints at that time. Since then we have compiled an introductory newsheet explaining all the fundamental ins and outs of the house, listing the rules and the reasoning behind them and using this to back up the verbal welcome and introduction. It can perhaps, seem bewildering and slightly frightening for a single person or young mother to be confronted with the thought of having to live in a hostel of this size without being given some guidance as to the layout and facilities. They also appreciate the reassurance that there are likely to be other people living alongside them who are probably experiencing similar circumstances. However, most individuals soon find their feet and begin to make friends or, as happened on more than one occasion, the shy young woman with the newborn baby turns out to be a completely different character from the one you were introduced to three weeks earlier. The following case illustrates the apparent change in character over a number of months and the difficulties involved in trying to help in such situations.

Ann

Ann came to the hostel when her baby was just a couple of weeks old. She appeared to be very shy and retiring, and did not mix with the other residents; when I managed to engage her in conversation she would avoid any direct eye contact. She was allocated one of the biggest rooms in the house as this was the only one empty at the time. Allocations are normally made by the council officers with little or no consultation with the wardens. Her boyfriend visited her frequently and he was often the one to come and query anything that Ann did not understand or was worried about. With his support she seemed to be coping reasonably well. Then it became apparent that the relationship was faltering, and when this first boyfriend disappeared from the scene he was quickly followed by a number of different male faces. There were rumours that Ann was not looking after the baby properly and would go out and leave him alone in the room. These reports, however, were unsubstantiated although I became increasingly concerned about the seemingly quick changeover of boyfriends. Officially residents are not permitted to have overnight visitors, although this 'rule' may be flexibly applied dependent on an individual's circumstances.

It soon became apparent that Ann's boyfriends must be staying overnight, although when questioned on this she would deny that it was the case. Various tactics were tried, from giving friendly advice to pointing out that if she did not comply with her tenancy agreement then she would run the risk of losing her accommodation. Nothing seemed to affect her behaviour, and she proceeded to carry on as before. She also neglected paying her bills, something which she had been very conscientious about initially. The baby could be heard crying frequently but he always looked bright and well cared for whenever he was seen in the house. However, because Ann seemed so unapproachable and was unwilling to talk either to myself or the other warden about the baby or her lifestyle, I decided to try and contact her health visitor. This, however, was easier said than done. Without knowing the GP's name (which I did not), in this area it is apparently impossible to match the appropriate health visitor to the baby. This appeared to make the situation into one of stalemate. I had no evidence that the baby was being mistreated or neglected: it was just a feeling based on remarks made by other residents and my own reaction to the girl's unwillingness to communicate. I felt I could not take the matter any further without firm evidence to support my claims. I suppose I was also worried that I was judging Ann on her behaviour with her numerous boyfriends rather than as a mother. Perhaps I was condemning her for behaviour I felt unable to condone; but I still felt concerned about the baby's welfare in what appeared to be unstable circumstances. Normally I would try and discuss with the resident the need for contacting outside assistance in the form of a social worker, health visitor or probation officer. However, in this case feeling unable to communicate with Ann, I sensed that any attempt to involve the 'authorities' would be seen by her as an intrusion.

Luckily, for me, I was able to assuage my conscience within a couple of weeks because a chance visit by a health visitor to see another resident resulted in the discovery that she was in fact Ann's too. I was able to relate my concern over the baby and was subsequently reassured that the health visitor was making regular visits and was aware of the situation. She in turn had some misgivings over the number of male friends Ann appeared to be associating with and confirmed that she found Ann was not an easy person to talk to; Ann had apparently refused offers to help from her family. I now had an 'official' to whom I could refer if the situation should cause me further concern, and a few weeks later I was impelled to do so. Much to our surprise – as she was in rent arrears – Ann was offered a temporary tenancy on a flat on the other side of the town. When the time came for her to move, she decided to go without informing either myself or the other warden, leaving not only all her keys with another resident but the baby too! We found out a day or so later and each time we questioned the other girl as to when Ann would be collecting the baby we were told a different story. When Ann failed to appear on the third day we decided that something had to be done and contacted both the housing department and the health visitor. However, in the midst of our discussions Nancy (who had been left with the baby) must have heard what was going on and took off with the child. On her return she informed us that she did not 'want any trouble' and had returned the baby to Ann, a fact confirmed later by the health visitor.

This case epitomizes many of the difficulties that can arise for young single mothers trying to cope alone and for those of us who have to try and ascertain exactly what the circumstances require. I did feel that I had somehow not done as much as I could, and on reflection perhaps a firmer approach at the start might have been beneficial to everyone; offering helpful advice is often regarded as interfering, whereas laying down strict guidelines in the beginning might have been exactly what was needed to contain the situation.

Nicki

Nicki was another resident who caused us a few headaches. She was a likeable young woman and, in contrast to Ann, was very outgoing and willing to talk over her 'problems' with any and everyone. Unfortunately, each time in the telling the problems and circumstances seemed to change. It took me a little while to realize the extent of her imagination, and it was only when I had to deny some of her stories to the other residents that I fully comprehended how much she liked to elaborate on the truth. When Nicki first came to us we had very little knowledge about her background, other than her age (nineteen), the fact that she was pregnant and that she did not get on with her family. It was soon obvious that she liked a lot of attention, and she would frequently come and knock at the flat door under one pretext or another. At times she could be very noisy, both by playing her music at a high level or just by talking in her loud voice. She was always quick to apologize, though, and willing to quieten down; it just never seemed to last very long. The other residents tolerated her 'stories' and in fact I think she was quite well liked. The real problems arose when she appeared to be miscarrying her baby. She had by all accounts already lost one baby this way and I was very anxious about her when she began having 'pains', and I urged her to contact her doctor immediately.

One day I came home in the middle of the afternoon to find Nicki waiting with a midwife for the ambulance to arrive, in all probability about to lose the baby. I was rather surprised to find her knocking at the door three hours later saying she had walked back from the hospital after having a miscarriage. Of course the hospital were unwilling to impart any information about what had happened and it was some days later before it was confirmed, unofficially, that Nicki had been suffering from a phantom pregnancy. A few weeks later she took an overdose of paracetamol but luckily informed another resident about what she had done, and we quickly got her to hospital. I must confess that I was appalled at the apparent lack of aftercare resulting from both these events, but could not really make out whether it was the system failing the individual or Nicki refusing any real help. However, the very fact that I was unable to trace the information has made me realize the need for better communication between the authorities.

Nicki seemed to bounce back after each incident, and indeed thrived on the attention she received; the tragedy of the situation now, some months hence, when she has been deemed by the council as intentionally homeless is that I hear she is pregnant again. I am left speculating whether or not her need is for a baby or for a place to live, and to get the latter it is necessary for her to have, or be about to produce, the former.

Ian

Ian was another nineteen-year-old resident who sought me out at every opportunity. He arrived one day with nothing but the clothes he was standing up in, and certainly in need of more help than we were equipped to offer him. He seemed to have very little idea about how to look after himself properly, but tried to cover up his inadequacies by telling elaborate stories about his background and current circumstances. In the past he had been in trouble with the police and later I learnt that he had a history of glue sniffing. One of the problems that manifested itself quite quickly was with his feet, from which emanated an awful smell. The other residents were very suspicious of him – as they tended to be of all single men living in the unit – and it was obvious he felt very isolated. One of the difficulties that we constantly face when trying to cope with 'vulnerable' residents is the lack of information that is passed on to us about each person and the seeming disinterest of those bodies who are meant to be offering supportive back-up. In recent months the involvement of the council has increased, with a housing officer being allocated to each Homeless Unit. This has enabled us to establish much more quickly which other agencies have, or need, to be involved in cases where problems arise. It has also provided a direct support system which was lacking when the hostel was first opened.

Ian would often wait for me late each evening as I was about to check the house for the night. He would usually question me about some trivial matter, but it was obvious he just wanted somebody to talk to. On other occasions he would go missing for a few days at a time, and once left his few belongings outside my flat with a note to say that he could not live at the unit anymore. He returned a couple of days later having changed his mind. I did feel sorry for Ian and spent a lot of time chatting to him; not, I am convinced, to any great effect, as he usually disregarded my suggestions. I also provided him with hot drinks and food on more than one occasion. This is something I usually try to avoid, except in an extreme situation, as I feel it may create conflict between the residents who, justifiably, can see it as one person being given special treatment. Ian, I think, needed far more support from the whole community, and when he eventually upped and left without a word to anyone I did feel that there may have been more that I could have done to help.

Sonia

One person Ian seemed to have a certain rapport with was Sonia, a woman in her late thirties who arrived in the house as a guest of another resident. She had recently been discharged from the local mental hospital and came to visit another of the ex-patients with whom she had become friendly. The only trouble was that she had nowhere else to go and, although at the time we had spare rooms, as wardens we are unable to allocate them. Eventually she was persuaded to apply to the homelessness team and was given temporary accommodation with us. When Sonia was in a good mood she was smart and articulate, but it gradually became obvious that she had been through some very traumatic experiences which had left her without a job, deprived her of her family and a home. Her mother and an elderly friend came to visit with grocery parcels from time to time, but Sonia seemed to be a very lonely woman. It was obvious, by her behaviour, that at times she turned to drink as a comfort and said she found it impossible to sleep without the aid of sleeping tablets. Things came to a head one Boxing Day night when another resident knocked at the flat to inform me that Sonia was wandering about half naked and very distressed. I spent all that night sitting with Sonia trying to keep her calm and stop her waking the other residents. Initially all she kept asking for was sleeping tablets, but as it appeared that she was not registered with a GP it was difficult trying to persuade a doctor to come and visit her in the middle of the night. The social worker on duty at the local hospital was unwilling to offer any help, apart from suggesting that I insist the doctor on call at the surgery she had visited as a temporary patient should attend her. At 5 a.m. he eventually agreed and administered some tablets; at last, I thought I can get some rest myself, but that was not to be. The sleeping tablets, if that is what they were, certainly did not work and Sonia's behaviour became even more agitated with her need for cigarettes becoming obsessional. I managed to dissuade her from waking any of the other residents to beg for them and kept the mugs of tea flowing and resigned myself to a night devoid of any sleep. Knowing that Sonia had once attempted suicide, by throwing herself under a car, I was worried that she might attempt the same again. I must confess that at times I found it hard to keep calm with Sonia and maintain a level head. If it had not been for my sympathetic partner who was able to take over from me at around 7 a.m. I am not sure how I would have coped. After a great deal of telephoning around – being Christmas time most of the official departments were still closed for the holidays – we were able to persuade the hospital to re-admit Sonia as a voluntary patient.

I had at one point in the night realized that I could have been in a potentially dangerous situation. I had no real understanding of the state of Sonia's mind, and certainly no professional training for coping in such a predicament. My feelings of inadequacy and isolation spurred me to try and establish if there were any provisions made for a back-up system in the event of a similar event occurring: I am still not convinced that it exists, but in my mind it certainly should.

Reflecting on experience

These examples illustrate just a small percentage of the number of cases that we have experienced over the past eighteen months. There are, of course, a fair number of residents who cause us no real problems, and from time to time there has been a rewarding sense of community spirit prevailing in the house. At the other end of the scale, however, we have also had to cope with situations where alcoholism, the use of drugs or violent relationships have exacerbated already volatile situations.

On reflection it occurs to me that I have probably depicted a rather negative assessment of life as a residential worker, but there are positive aspects too. There are those people who come to the unit in a very despondent mood, expecting the place to be dismal and unfriendly, and who express unmasked relief that both the house and the warden are far better than they expected. These are often the people who may come to the office for a chat, and in the course of conversation ask for help with their financial or emotional problems, or some advice about a child's behaviour. If these residents stay with us for any length of time it is probable that the relationship can develop into a friendly one. The danger then, which I have so far managed to avoid, is in becoming too close to a resident and therefore unable to exert an authoritative attitude when necessary. It is when these residents leave that I tend to experience conflicting emotions: there is pleasure that they are being moved on to more suitable accommodation, but a kind of sadness that a friendly face is disappearing from the scene.

The experience of being 'on-the-job' twenty-four hours a day affects not only me as a worker but also my partner and family. Living just down the corridor from my work has the advantage that there's no traffic to negotiate first thing in the morning and no getting wet if it is pouring with rain. For the residents, though, it sometimes makes it all too easy for them to forget that I have a life that is separate from the homeless unit. There have been times when some of the residents seem to feel that they have a right to disturb me, at any time of the day or night, however trivial the problem. It is surprising, too, how persistent, and infuriating, someone's knocking can be when I have just got into that nice, hot and (what was meant to be) relaxing bath. Another disconcerting aspect is the knowledge that the argument I have just had with my partner or the telling off I have just administered, yet again, to one of my children was probably heard by at least half-a-dozen residents whose rooms are in close proximity to my flat. I have come to realize, though, that my children do not appear to share my concern about their behaviour being 'on view'. They do occasionally mix with the children in the hostel, but as my sons tend to be older than them and my baby daughter not yet at the age of playing without Mummy being close by, the contact is usually minimal. I do try to keep my job separate from my family, and although my sons have a natural curiosity about what is happening in the house I try not to make specific comments about residents in front of them. For my partner it is rather different as, from time to time, he can be directly involved with the residents. He realizes, though, that the information he may learn about residents or the discussions we have when I need to let off steam are strictly confidential.

Apart from the residents there are other people who also seem to find it difficult to respect the privacy of time. Repair people and housing officers seem to turn up or phone even when they should be aware of my official duty hours. They can become quite annoyed when this is pointed out to them and it is difficult trying to remain resolute about adhering to duty hours when I am aware that if I refuse entry to the plumbers, for example, the job they have come to do might then get left for a couple of weeks or more. There also seems to be an unspoken assumption that if my partner is around, even though I may be out, he will comply with any requests from the residents or council. A recent example of how problems can arise occurred when I had to go into hospital for an emergency operation late one Friday afternoon. I just had time to phone into the council offices, before they closed for the weekend, and leave a message for my boss; I stuck a notice on the office door with an explanatory message and left for the hospital. On my return a few days later, even though we had placed a notice on the flat door explaining the situation and asking not to be disturbed, several people ignored this request and came to us with their problems. Obviously it was left to my partner, who was trying to look after both me and our nine-month-old baby daughter, to cope with these interruptions and try to impress on the residents that they would have to wait for the deputy warden to come on duty. I think at that particular time I found it more infuriating than he did, but on other occasions we have had disagreements when I have chosen to sort a problem out when it is meant to be my time off; which goes to prove that unless you actually go out or away when you are not on duty it can be very difficult to relax.

In assessing this type of work it must be remembered that there is no 'typical' homeless person; age, health, family and financial circumstances will all be different, as will the way in which each individual learns to cope with being classed as homeless. I have found that, not surprisingly, it is usually the single young person who often appears to be the loneliest and in need of the most support. Some residential hostels are aimed specifically at young people and will subsequently be equipped with both the staff and facilities beneficial to their lifestyles. In contrast, the few older residents that have been placed with us have hardly had enough time to adjust to hostel living as they have been moved to other accommodation within a few weeks. The single mothers or families with small children usually mix quite well, but living as closely as they do with one another can bring problems with over-familiarity and intrusions into privacy.

Trying to maintain the equilibrium is certainly the priority within the house, and offering advice and support for each individual's needs is another crucial aspect of the job. At times I have been frustrated by the lack of consideration some residents have shown towards those around them, and at others by officials who seem unable, or unwilling, to respond to requests for help, either for myself or a resident. Part of the challenge of the job is in trying to combat these inadequacies. The resulting satisfaction that can be felt when a small triumph is achieved is what keeps me going. It is not easy to assess the value of this type of residential work. Assisting people to cope with being homeless is the greatest need, and if this is achieved then any further interventions by me which result in someone's personal development are a bonus. Working 'in residence' requires patience and understanding, and also the ability to define living and working boundaries and the strength of character to achieve a satisfactory compromise between the two. If this is accomplished then working in a people-orientated environment can be both stimulating and satisfying.

Questions for consideration

1 There are some obvious and not so obvious drawbacks to 'living on the job'. What would you envisage as being the main disadvantages, and how could you adjust to living with them?
2 Faced with the problem of an unco-operative resident whose behaviour is giving cause for concern to both residents and warden, how would you pursue the objectives of obtaining the resident's co-operation and restoring harmony to the hostel?
3 If you felt that the back-up you were receiving from your organization was inadequate, how would you attempt to change the situation?
4 In the event of a major catastrophe, i.e., fire, flooding or bomb scare in the middle of the night, what would be your priorities and how would you deal with it?
5 If a couple of residents were persistently leaving communal areas in a filthy state:
    (a) How would you track down who was responsible?
    (b) What steps would you take in trying to stop the problem recurring?

7

Advising and Advocacy

LYNNZIE STIRLING

Social workers give a great deal of advice. It is not always fashionable for them to admit that this is the case. Such behaviour appears to fly in the face of a commitment to the 'empowerment' and 'self-actualization' of clients. Because of the vague aura of guilt often pervading the activity, little discussion has occurred regarding the most appropriate and effective ways of undertaking it. This is a pity for not only do many clients seek it, but it is also often incumbent upon social workers to provide good advice. Advocacy is a much more widely acknowledged activity. It is far more acceptable, perhaps because it appears to represent a positive form of intervention at the behest of the client; it appears to place social workers unambiguously on the side of the under-privileged.

This chapter links these two activities through exploring the values which should connect them, and indicating how advice might lead to different forms of advocacy. Lynnzie Stirling suggests that both activities can be used to enhance the control which clients exercise over their own lives. What appears crucial is that we as workers are clear about our roles and honest with our clients. Both of these are familiar themes from earlier chapters. This chapter also indicates, as did Jeremy Walker, the importance of examining and relating to the subjective experience of each client. Even though circumstances may be familiar, the worker must avoid producing an 'off the peg' solution. Along with this goes avoiding imposing our own solutions on our clients.

This is, of course, sometimes easier said than done because it can conflict with our wish to do our best for our clients. There are, however, limitations on simply standing back and allowing clients to make their own decisions. The examples given here (showing, for instance, the resistance which may initially be encountered), indicate that questions of when to give and when to withhold advice, when to persuade and when to back away are complex professional judgments. Readers will be prompted to look at examples of all of these in their own work.

Advocacy brings with it a need for careful consideration of relationships with other agencies. Is it possible to work in collaboration with other agencies whilst at the same time being an advocate for one's client who is in conflict with them? Through case examples Lynnzie shows the difficult path that each social worker needs to tread if a careful balance between different sets of relationships is to be maintained.

Both advice-giving and advocacy assume that social workers possess a reservoir of knowledge upon which to draw and the skills to research and acquire expertise in the interests of their client. Lynnzie shows that social workers need to take deliberate and practical steps to build up even a rudimentary data base of useful information. Community care makes this an even more pertinent issue. We are also prompted to think once again about teamwork and how collective working of some kind might most efficiently collate and accumulate useful information and resources. Similarly, we may also be prompted to think about the way our own advocacy on behalf of our clients can be expanded and enhanced. In particular, issues of collective advocacy are likely to be raised as a result of reading and discussing this chapter.

* * *

The key principle in both advising and advocacy is that the social worker always works in such a way as to allow clients the maximum degree of power over their own decisions and choices. It should naturally follow that advice and advocacy should always be carried out in such a way as to enhance, rather than detract from or undermine, clients' competence to direct their own lives.

The social worker can offer the client suggestions about alternative actions, but the decision to act must be the client's. Having made a decision, the client may then need guidance and/or support in taking effective action which may lead to advocacy.

In other words, having decided on the course of action, the client may, or may not, have the necessary skills and resources to follow this through. They may therefore need some degree of advocacy, meaning more than just advice: maybe someone speaking on their behalf, or in other ways assisting them to pursue their cause. Ideally guidance or support should leave them better able to act for themselves in future.

At this point, it might be helpful to make it clear that what I shall be discussing in this chapter is akin to what normally goes under the title of 'professional advocacy'. The term 'advocacy' currently embraces a number of different roles, the main ones being:

(a) 'professional advocacy' concerns a paid worker, ideally employed by an independent organization, charged with the task of acting and speaking on behalf of a client to obtain the form of service required by that individual;

(b) 'citizen advocacy' involves the use of trained volunteers who work on a one-to-one basis with clients (typically those with disabilities or who otherwise might be disadvantaged in representing themselves) in order to defend and promote their rights and dignity;

(c) 'self-advocacy' refers to situations in which people represent themselves in a fairly formal way, although they may have support from others in developing the relevant skills to do this;

(d) 'legal advocacy' describes a wide range of methods and activities by which lawyers and others with legal training help people exercise their rights under law;

(e) 'collective/class/structural advocacy' is where people join together, sometimes under the banner of an organization, to campaign at a political level on issues which affect a particular group or class of people such as those with disabilities or the homeless (Butler, Carr and Sullivan, 1988; Card, 1990).

Martin Davies describes the qualities that make for a good advocate in social work;

he is likely to be a natural leader with a strong personality and expertise in his subject; he will be knowledgeable and have his facts right; he will be politically adept, knowing which are the appropriate leverage points to bring about change; he will be known for his professional integrity; and he will be capable of presenting his client's case forcefully and efficiently. Khan found that workers needing to have constant recourse to team meetings or to consult with colleagues did not make good advocates: the practitioners of sound advocacy programmes were found to be more self reliant and autonomous than other social workers. (Davies, 1985, p. 68)

Advocacy not only requires accumulated knowledge and experience of a particular area, but also access to considerable time and resources. Also it is often fitted alongside routine social work. Logically, it may well be prudent to start at an individual level, if only because penalties for failure are likely to be greater at a structural level.

The social worker as adviser

Almost anyone can find themselves in a position of seeking or giving advice. People with problems or difficulties may have the choice of going to a whole range of lay and professional advice-givers. In what ways does the social worker's role as adviser differ from that of a relative or neighbour?

One reason why someone seeks advice from a professional such as a social worker rather than a friend or relative is because they see professionals as authoritative. This places a responsibility on the latter to be clear about, and to make clear to their clients, the boundaries between advice based on professional expertise and that based on personal experience.

Each client will also have his or her own individual expectations when seeking the advice of a social worker. Not all of these will necessarily be expressed at the outset. It is the responsibility of the social worker to clarify with the client what these expectations are and to agree which ones they are prepared to meet. This may sometimes require negotiation and will be based on judgments of what the social worker can realistically provide given their professional and personal competences, as well as what is in the client's best interest.

The social worker should be in a better position than the non-professional to know where to find relevant information and to package this is such a way as to ensure that it will be accurate, unbiased, acceptable and capable of being followed. In all this a key issue is confidentiality. I will say more about accuracy later. Initially I will concentrate on the other issues.

The temptations of collusion

Joan was in her mid-twenties and living with her divorced mother on the same housing estate as her elder married brother and two married sisters. Apart from her work on the checkout of a local supermarket Joan had little social life; she spent most of her time looking after nieces and nephews and supporting other family members. She presented as the family drudge.

Joan was admitted to hospital suffering from severe anxiety and depression, the main apparent cause of her state being long-term familial discord and habitual rows. As well as being treated as the family work horse, Joan was the butt of much verbal abuse. She appeared to be totally lacking in self-esteem and presented as a hapless victim. She was at a crossroads, knowing that she could not go on any longer but not knowing what to do to change things.

During the course of my discussions with Joan and other significant family members it became clear that there were faults on all sides. However, Joan appeared to want to maintain a particular image of herself as the victim. She tried to do this by quoting comments made by friends and her checkout supervisor regarding her mother, brother and sisters: 'My friend knows what they're like'; 'My boss says I shouldn't put up with them, I should move away': 'My friends never liked my family.'

However, it had become clear in the few weeks I had known Joan that she had deceived her family about debts she had accumulated, and she had told complex lies to different family members. I felt I had to confront Joan with the possibility that there was some connection between her deception and the behaviour of her family towards her.

Whilst I respected Joan's right to make her own decision about whether or not to leave both the area and her family, I felt it would not be helpful to future relationships if she made such a decision without acknowledging her part in the familial discord.

Joan's reaction to my suggestion was to become very angry with me and emotionally upset to such a degree that I had to conclude the interview. However, on seeing her the next day I found her willing to admit, albeit grudgingly, that there might be some truth in what I had said.

It would have made for an easier interview had I colluded with Joan in her view that the family was all wrong and she was all right. To reinforce her view of the situation with biased advice would not have served her best interests. It is important for social workers to understand their role in the advice-giving process and to have a very clear notion as to why their advice is equal to, or of greater worth than, anyone else's.

The client comes to the social worker expecting 'good' advice. However, good advice is not always what the client wishes to hear.

The difficulties in accepting advice

There is often a need to employ social work skills to prepare the ground for the person to accept advice and support. For example, writing to make an appointment; making it at a convenient time and place according to what is known of the client's situation; being ordinary and pleasant; acknowledging previous approaches; and respecting the client's right to refuse but not making this an excuse for no action, especially in 'difficult' cases. It is important to distinguish between a client not wanting advice and not being ready to accept it. In the latter situation the social worker's preparatory behaviour can make a crucial difference.

Terry, a 43-year-old divorced man, had suffered a stroke when he was 35 years old and had moved back to live with his elderly mother. Physically he had recovered fairly well. However, refusal to accept speech therapy had resulted in his speech remaining severely impaired. Terry was known to be subject to mood changes and slight disagreements with his mother could cause violent aggressive outbursts. He was also known to be a misuser of both alcohol and cannabis to excess.

When his mother suffered a heart attack Terry was referred to us for support, counselling and assessment for independent living. He had been referred to the department several times before and, from the file, I could see that various options and support had been offered over the years. He had steadfastly refused all offers of help or support. His family were unaware of this and had felt that the social workers had just not bothered to do anything.

Having read the file, I made contact with his brother in order to get an up-to-date picture of the situation and discuss the best time to call on Terry. I wrote and made an appointment but when I called Terry was still in bed and, with the liberal use of Anglo-Saxon language, made it clear that he did not want to see me. Following this, I rang his brother and said I would call in 'on spec' some time.

When I did eventually call back, Terry greeted me with some surprise and amusement, confessing that he had not expected to see me again after the verbal abuse. This time he was in a calmer frame of mind and was able to accept some support, albeit limited.

I might have been justified in taking Terry's first reaction as a clear indication that he did not want social work support, but the reaction to my second visit showed that, in fact, he found it difficult to accept such support.

There are occasions when the client comes for advice but has a hidden agenda of actually wanting the social worker to make the decisions. If the latter offers the client an analysis of their situation and a range of options as to how to change things, together with support through the change process, the client may well go away feeling they have not been helped or advised at all.

Offering relevant advice

Social workers need to be committed to the service they are offering and prepared to be persistent in order to hold out opportunities for the client to accept help.

It is important to remember our clients are individuals, and not a set of categories. They are not simply 'like the people down the road', 'people with problems', 'people we've known in the past'. We must guard against projecting images on to them based on preconceived ideas or even referral information. We must be prepared to look beyond first presentations. The key thing is to actively listen to the client: you have never 'heard it all before'.

Social workers are prone to the same kind of errors as everyone else in terms of their judgments about people. We all hold what psychologists have called 'implicit personality theories' (Schneider, 1973). You do not stop being a person just because you are a social worker and you do not stop being a social worker just because you are 'off duty'. Self-awareness is important.

It is easy to give advice based on what we ourselves are comfortable with rather than on an objective appreciation of the client's situation. Our advice needs to be tailored to the particular client and not generalized.

John, a man in his early forties and recently registered blind, referred himself to the social services department for housing advice. He lived alone and was supported by his younger sister, Carol, who lived some distance from him. John and Carol wished to live together with Carol's young daughter and sought help and support in their negotiations with the housing department to exchange their one- and two-bedroomed flats for a three-bedroomed house.

The housing department were sympathetic to the situation and would readily have offered John and Carol a joint tenancy within a matter of weeks had it not been for Carol's rent arrears. The housing department were bound by their rules and would not consider a transfer until the arrears of £240 were cleared. Finding £240 was a major problem and several possible options were considered.

1 Pay off the arrears at £20 per week (£10 each). This was unacceptable due to the length of time it would take to clear the arrears when both Carol and John felt the need to move was now urgent.
2 Apply for a Department of Social Security (DSS) loan. Carol pointed out the time factor again, since an application for a DSS loan can be many weeks in the pipeline and can then still be refused. Carol also felt that if she had a DSS loan she would not have the control she would like over her money since the repayments are taken at source.
3 John should give up his tenancy and move in with Carol and her daughter and use his rent to pay off the arrears. This was rejected by both of them because of the time taken to clear the debt owing to the reduction in his DSS payments were he to 'live in' with his sister. Also, their relationship might suffer if they were living in cramped conditions.
4 John should borrow the money from a local man who runs such a business on the estate. Carol and John thought this was the best idea but I broke out in an cold sweat at the very thought of contacting a loan shark!

After some time of what I took to be supportive discussion (manoeuvring John and Carol from the private loan option because I was fearful of the consequences of any default on the repayments), I was quite suddenly aware that I had not actually been listening to John at all because I was too busy listening to me!

When I did hear what John was saying it was clear that he had frequently used this type of loan before and had always managed very well. He had sometimes even repaid the loan ahead of schedule and had received a small discount into the bargain. A private loan was the usual method John employed when he was faced with the problem of finding a large sum of money all at once. John and Carol could cope with 'loan sharks'; it was the social worker who had a problem with them!

A short time later a private loan of £240 was secured and the rent arrears were cleared. The housing transfer was completed and the loan subsequently repaid, all without difficulty.

Advice should be tempered with a judgment of what the client is capable of, given support. It is easy to cover yourself by saying you have given the advice even if the client fails to act on it successfully, but this cannot be ethically acceptable.

Confidentiality

Social workers will naturally be aware that confidentiality is an important ethical issue. However, in the situation where you are the client's adviser or advocate there are also practical considerations. The fact that information given by the client will be classed as highly confidential needs to be stressed to them. The main reason for this is that we shall be offering advice on the information we are given, and if the client keeps information back for fear of a breach of confidentiality then we may be giving advice in the absence of significant information. It is helpful to explain this to the client, at the same time as outlining the necessary limits of confidentiality.

Advocacy

Being a successful advocate means being competent to speak in a given area. Confidence should not be confused with competence.

Hilda, a 44-year-old sufferer from myasthenic encephalitis (ME), was in dispute with the DSS over the withdrawal of her mobility allowance. She asked me to attend the appeals tribunal with her. Although I was quite happy to accompany her in a supportive role, Hilda wanted me to speak on her behalf. This was something outside my experience and, whilst I felt confident about doing it, I was not sure about my competence.

I advised Hilda that, although I was happy to accompany her, I felt she would be better served if she were represented by a welfare rights worker. She accepted my advice and engaged a welfare rights worker, but we also agreed that I would go along both to support her and to extend my own knowledge and experience in the appeals procedure.

If social workers do not feel competent in a particular area, they should at least know where to direct their client. A telephone call or letter in support of the referral can be helpful to those to whom you pass the client.

Whilst I have been restricting myself to issues concerned with professional advocacy, it needs to be emphasized that any act of advocacy by a social worker should aim to move clients towards greater self-advocacy. Advocacy means not just stopping at advice-giving but going with clients along the route of implementing the advice in such a way as to offer them maximum control at each stage.

Advocacy, in these terms, sometimes approaches a kind of behaviour shaping, although it is not a behaviour modification programme. Rather, it is a state of mind; a constant sensitivity to opportunities for helping clients to act on their own behalf whilst attempting to ensure positive outcomes for them in the short term.

Valerie, a 38-year-old woman with learning disabilities, recently moved away from her mother's care to live alone in the community. She suffers from epilepsy and sought my help in purchasing a cover to save her mattress from being spoiled should she be incontinent at night during an epileptic fit.

I was able to offer Valerie the telephone numbers of three local retailers who might possibly supply her with the cover she needed and stayed with her whilst she made her own telephone enquiries about prices and stock availability. Valerie was able to make the decision that she would call and inspect the covers at a shop, and asked me to accompany her for general support.

Before going to the shop both Valerie and I had a very clear idea regarding the level of support and advice I would be offering. In essence she was on her own and I would only intervene should her dignity be at risk.

All went well for Valerie until the shop assistant offered a choice of two mattress covers, the first being a full cover 'generally bought by people suffering from allergic rhinitis', as the assistant told her, and the second 'usually bought by those who experience nocturnal enuresis'. Valerie and I looked at each other, with expressions fit to bust! Valerie turned back to the assistant and expressed her need to think things over.

I explained the meaning of the two unfamiliar terms to Valerie and made strenuous attempts not to lead Valerie in her choice mattress cover. The options were open and the choice remained entirely hers.

In this case, it might have saved a lot of time and effort just to have made the choice for her, but this would have left her less equipped to make similar decisions in future.

In acting as advocates social workers need a degree of self-awareness. They need to be aware of how their own needs, or pressures from their own and other agencies, might impinge on their advocacy role. Often there is pressure to collude with other agencies, resulting in divided loyalties.

Not infrequently, local authority social workers and officers from other agencies, with whom they are involved on behalf of the client, share the same employer. How much freedom do social workers have at the end of the day, and how do they deal with such situations? Are there any rules of thumb (e.g., should the client's needs always take precedence)? The social worker has to take some stance and make a judgment: 'The social worker cannot be an arbitrary dispenser of justice unique to the needs of one family irrespective of others. He can act as an advocate on behalf of the family but he cannot claim absolute priority for them merely because they are his clients' (Davies, 1985, p. 155).

Barry's situation was involved and complicated, eventually culminating in a direction from the Ombudsman to the local housing department that they should offer him single person accommodation. Unlike me, the housing department had known Barry for several years and saw him as a difficult client. They were not motivated to do any more than the minimum to comply with the Ombudsman's directive.

I went to see how things were going in terms of finding Barry a place and was conscious of a real pressure to conform to the widely shared negative view of Barry or else risk alienating myself, perhaps to the detriment of future clients. I had to steer a middle ground between maintaining my own and my client's integrity. Whilst social workers are free to compromise themselves, they should never compromise their clients in order to achieve what they want. Experiences like this point to the need to spend time building relationships with, and gaining the respect of, other agencies in preparation for advocacy. As Davies says: 'there is no doubt that social workers do act as advocates, but their ability to do so successfully almost certainly depends on them being accepted as at least relatively impartial' (Davies, 1985, p. 89).

Social workers need to operate both strategically and tactically. The former means investing time in building relationships and extending one's knowledge, whilst the latter involves the use of social work skills in working with individual clients. Time needs to be put aside for developing one's resources as a social worker, and I shall say more about this later.

Encouraging self-advocacy

It is important that social workers restrict their involvement to the minimum regarding both advice-giving and advocacy. It can be easy to reinforce dependency but this does not help the client in the long term, and neither does it help the social worker who can all too easily become overloaded with work.

It is necessary to be alert to opportunities for helping the client to learn strategies for self-direction. This means being ready to share knowledge and decision-making skills with them. Underpinning all this is the need to respect and value the client and their capacity for self-determination. If social workers fail to do this then there is a risk that the system becomes silted up with long-term clients, leaving little time free for new cases. You have to let people go.

Enhancing advocacy

A social worker should not pretend to be a lawyer; however, a basic knowledge of relevant law is fundamental to social work practice. Social workers do not necessarily need a detailed knowledge of the law, but they do need to know that there is relevant legislation. (An excellent guide to the law can be found in Brayne and Martin, 1991.)

Social workers are rarely expected to be so generic these days. However, whilst they should have a thorough working knowledge of the legislation relevant to their own specialism, they should also have a basic understanding of legislation appropriate to other areas of social work. It is all too easy to think you know, and so hard to say you do not, especially when people are looking to you for advice. Social workers have to function in the role of both specialist and general practitioner whilst being aware of their professional boundaries and personal limitations.

Another important issue is the acquisition of strategies for gathering and storing the information on which your advice is based. It is sensible to invest time in preparing your systems beforehand so that you are ready to begin storing information from the first day. Prior to starting a new post social workers should go through their files and sort out the things that are likely to be useful on a day-to-day basis. Once in post there are some items of basic equipment that can prove very helpful. Some suggestions would be:

- A telephone book, preferably a ring binder type to make additions and subtractions easier
- A file box for keeping copies of articles and other information relevant to your particular client group
- An index card file for details of local establishments (day centres, hostels, bed and breakfast, etc.), both public and private. It is useful to include here notes about the personnel in these establishments in order to help in building relations
- A 'duty file' which comprises your copy of all the relevant information and documentation that might be needed as duty social worker. You cannot always rely on being readily available in the duty room

From the outset the social worker should develop the habit of systematically recording and storing information with a view to easy retrieval. Time invested in storing information properly saves time and frustration later when it is needed.

Be eager and thirsty for information and proactive in acquiring knowledge. For example, any time you ask for a potentially useful telephone number, or even hear one mentioned, write it in the book. Read professional journals on a regular basis and store information that might be useful. Develop the habit of glancing through the local papers to get a flavour of the area, and use the local library's 'what's on' noticeboard. Be an active listener (for example, to what colleagues talk about). Share information with, and learn from, colleagues. Make use of things like team meetings as sources of information and take the opportunity to chat to people without feeling that you are wasting time.

It is vital that your information is accurate. This means spending time updating it. The social worker has an absolute duty to ensure that any advice given is accurate since if it is not it can be more damaging than offering no advice.

It is possible to go beyond individual advocacy by becoming a member of a particular local group which campaigns on behalf of clients. MIND and the Alzheimers Disease Society are two which come to mind, but there are many others. Joining a society or a group serves the additional function of keeping the social worker's advising and advocacy data base up to date (a necessary process).

There is the ongoing need for social workers to advocate on behalf of social work itself. This can be with colleagues and other professionals or on a more personal and local basis with friends and neighbours and 'down the pub'. It is only reasonable to expect social workers to represent their profession effectively.

Finally, it is important to cultivate efficiency and to 'look the part'. The appearance projected by social workers says a lot about how they value their clients and their professional credibility. As one young man commented when asked what he thought of his social worker: 'He's OK, but he doesn't half dress scruffy.'

Conclusions

A key principle in both advising and advocacy is that social workers should always strive to operate in such a way as to allow their clients the maximum degree of power over their own decisions and choices. Advice and advocacy should always be carried out in such a way as to enhance, rather than subtract from, or undermine, clients' ability to direct their own lives.

Questions for consideration

1 What are the differences and similarities in giving advice as a social worker and giving advice as a friend or relative?
2 Does giving advice automatically undermine client autonomy?
3 Do social workers have a professional responsibility to offer support to those organizations campaigning for better conditions for their clients?
4 How are advice and advocacy roles changing in relation to community care?
5 Is self-advocacy merely a hoped-for ideal? How common are actual examples of it being achieved in practice?

References

Brayne, H. and G. Martin (1991) *Law for Social Workers* (2nd edn). London: Blackstone Press.

Butler, K., S. Carr and F. Sullivan (1988) *Citizen Advocacy: A Powerful Partnership*. London: National Citizen Advocacy.

Card, H. (1990) *Advocacy on Behalf of Elderly People with Mental Health Problems: A Report Based on a Six Month Pilot Project in Hove, East Sussex.* Brighton: Brighton Mental Health Project.

Davies, M. (1985) *The Essential Social Worker*. Aldershot: Gower.

Schneider, D. J. (1973) 'Implicit Personality Theory', *Psychological Bulletin*, 79, 294–309.

8

Educating

IRENE BOYD AND JANE SKITTRALL

Education is obviously the responsibility of teachers. Most other welfare professionals seem reluctant to label even a small part of their work as teaching. Youth and community workers, most health professionals and social workers all appear to shy away from being described as teachers; perhaps because it is viewed as authoritarian, patronizing and classroom based. Yet social workers, whatever the setting, frequently engage in what might be seen as educational dialogue with individuals and groups. Reluctance to acknowledge that social workers are educators has led to a failure to consider the value of teaching as a mode of intervention.

By making visible and examining their practice Irene Boyd and Jane Skittrall explore the value of combining an educational role with more familiar social work techniques. Contrary to expectations, rather than extending professional control and authority, this chapter suggests that educational approaches can be employed to raise the self-image and confidence of clients. Most social workers recognize the value of educational programmes in their own development and can use this experience to begin to bring similar benefits to their clients. It is important to recognize, in this context, that poverty has frequently severely limited the educational opportunities of those who become social work clients. This does not mean that they cannot benefit from opportunities for learning. The value of adopting an educational role need not be confined to 'low risk' settings. The cases cited here include work with groups who often give social workers the greatest cause for professional concern.

Building on the recognition of social workers as advice-givers, we begin to see in this chapter how one might go beyond this to develop the sort of dialogue which is neces-sary for educational relationships. Irene and Jane show that this depends on recognizing and valuing their client's own experience and knowledge and on seeing them as learners. Like Jeremy Walker and Deborah Marshall, they realize that this does not mean that situations always work out in an ideal way. Once again we see that solutions to problems have to arise from enhanced understanding on the part of clients themselves rather than being what the workers would consider the tidiest option.

By using groupwork, workers can enable participants to learn from each other. Examples are given here of situations where this kind of peer learning has been possible. Irene and Jane also acknowledge that they too have learnt a lot from these encounters. Their learning has not always been com-fortable as they began to understand the ways in which some clients experience social work intervention.

Educating is the least recognized of the various social work processes which are discussed in this book. Most of us will have hardly thought about what might be gained from seeing social work in this way. This chapter shows that we are only at the beginning, in this country, of what may well be a fruitful direction for our thinking about social work. Irene Boyd and Jane Skittrall argue that what is involved is a way of 'thinking and being' as educators rather than a set of tech-niques and principles. This is very much in keeping with the way we are all writing about practice in this book, but the focus on educating offers new and stimulating possibilities.

* * *

It is often a struggle to work with people in an educative way. The people we work with do not always wish to be educated or acquire knowledge (Rogers, 1983; Mullender and Ward, 1991). Many are reluctant to be offered 'help' in whatever form it takes and do not wish for social work intervention in their lives. Often the primary focus for intervention follows a crisis situation, such as a non-accidental injury which has been dealt with initially on a duty basis by one worker and has been thereafter allocated for assessment on a short- or long-term basis. Being honest about our intended involvement and the part that we will play in this can set the scene for a solid casework approach, and can assist learning and the transfer of information. Acknowledgment by a parent, for example, that there is a need for learning is an integral part of this process.

At one level, the educative process can be the simple transfer of information and knowledge which is perhaps one of the core activities of social work practice. At a very basic level, informing someone of their entitlement to claim, for example, family credit and how they make an application for it is transferring knowledge. Giving out information is easy and, provided that it is correct, it is a useful way of enabling clients to learn.

There are limitations, however, in attempting to achieve change through information-giving within a casework framework. There is always the danger of ignoring the context, and the meaning of the advice to those receiving it. We might show people how to be good parents, for example, through playing with their six-month-old baby. But how would this be received in a situation where, in addition to their six-month-old baby there is an eight-year-old child who behaves aggressively in the classroom; a ten-year-old child who steals and will not attend school; a husband involved in criminal activities; and a young mother herself with a history of being sexually abused and suffering from health problems? We know of such a family. Our team worked with them over a number of years. The concerns for their children were substantial enough to mean registration on the child protection register and the compulsory involvement of a social worker. The family continued to deny the need for these. The needs of this one family typify the complex range of issues within families with whom we work. Working with this family has also meant dealing with the anxieties of other professionals. There have been several requests for the children to be removed and accommodated by the local authority. These anxieties stem from the children appearing at school inappropriately dressed and hungry, as well as the high number of injuries to them.

The usual social services approach to this family would involve monitoring the children, guiding and instructing the parents and being providers as the need arose. There would be substantial pressure to respond to the accidental injuries in the home. This family had been the subject of numerous case conferences where it was acknowledged that the local authority had sufficient information to instigate legal proceedings.

As an alternative to this, we worked with this family in an educative way. This meant striking a balance between recognizing the statutory involvement of the department and the desire to achieve independence for this family. We found that this necessitated seeing the parents as learners which in turn involved a greater degree of voluntary participation. Working in this way returned some element of control to the parents. Both had been reluctant to work with social workers, given their own experiences of being received into care and their anxieties about a repeat of this for their children.

We engaged the parents in an intensive process which gave credence to their own experiences. We met weekly and at these times talked about their upbringing and their own understanding of their lives. Through this process, the parents began to use their knowledge to understand what their children were doing and why. During these weeks, the parents took an increasing amount of responsibility for what was being discussed and began to enter into dialogue with us. (Similar processes occurred in Gertig's (1990) account of work with carers.) We carefully encouraged them to use the responsibility that they were demonstrating in some areas of their lives, in particular in their parenting. This process was not smooth and continuous. There were often difficulties in engaging the parents, and there was a tendency for them to avoid issues. It was relatively easy to engage the parents' interests in the play and development of the children. For example, Mum began to watch the two youngest children and comment on their 'little ways'. We found that if the parents could watch what the children were doing, they were more inclined to interact with them. An incident occurred when one of the younger children was helping us to mend our notepad. Dad spontaneously joined in. This was the beginning of the parents becoming more involved in the children's play and has continued with the young children of this family. Learning for these parents took place in a non-threatening environment which was always their home. The parents determined how much knowledge they wanted and were able to engage us as workers in areas which concerned them. What we were trying to do was to work with the parents' own experiences and understandings. We were not attempting to interpret these from our own point of view, and neither were we expecting them to 'work through' their feelings. Rather we were, through our conversations, trying to create an environment in which they could deepen their own understanding, at a pace they could control. On this basis they were able to try out different ways of being with their children.

Education for independence

Education for independence involves an element of risk-taking as there are often tensions between the need to educate and the need to protect. When working with young people who are moving into independent living, the learning and negotiating process will have been an important element during their time spent in a residential establishment and will continue when they leave care. Everyday activities, such as shopping with a limited income and budgeting, provide an opportunity for learning to make judgments and choices.

We worked with one young woman over a period of two years. She had been received into care when she was 13 years old. Her parents would only have her returned home when her behaviour improved. Numerous attempts were made at rehabilitation. She overdosed on three occasions. Her behaviour became difficult and escalated to such a level that she became a management problem and violent within the residential home. She became involved in criminal activity and her whereabouts were often unknown. Clearly this young woman's emotional needs had not been met. Attempts were made during her period in care to engage her in therapeutic work, but her unstable lifestyle meant that this was not achieved.

This woman reappeared at the office after a long period of sleeping rough. By this time she was 17 years old, she was trying to face up to one more rejection from her parents and was asking to be received into care. Our social services department could have chosen to accept her once more into a residential home, interpreting that what she really needed was to be nurtured and cared for. However, it was felt more appropriate that she should be supported in a move to independent living. This decision was reached between the woman and ourselves after numerous discussions about what 'care' could offer her and her changing needs.

Working with this woman proved to be difficult. What we needed to do was to be able to work with her in a way which would allow her to achieve her goals successfully, one of which was establishing a secure base. The task of the worker was to help create the conditions and context to allow learning to occur. Initially we had to take on what appeared to be a parenting role, as this woman obviously needed to be cared for and be able to develop trust. This enabled us to communicate with her about her feelings and anxieties without creating dependency. During the contact we had with this woman, we concentrated on helping her to move into a flat, to make it comfortable, to organize her benefits, to budget and to live by herself. Throughout this, we would talk with her, challenge her and give support. She was often disinterested and was not able to manage her home. Some weeks when we met her in her flat, she was cold, hungry and despondent. She would ask for money, as this was what she had come to expect from social workers during her earlier years. It took many months for this expectation to change. She began to value contact with us. She was able to negotiate on her own behalf with agencies by being assertive rather than aggressive, and had more confidence in herself as a person.

We recognized that progress had been made in her moves to independence. However, this was not straightforward and brought other challenges. She became increasingly involved in offending with a group of friends. Eventually she terminated her tenancy. She stopped visiting the office and we were unable to continue working with her, despite attempts to find her. We now believe her to be living with a family in the area and she is expecting her first child. It is likely that we shall see this woman again at the office over the next few months.

Learning through groupwork

Groupwork within a social services area team is sometimes perceived as a method of working which should be undertaken by social workers in addition to their existing caseloads. Whilst innovative and successful groupwork projects are commended, those social workers permitted to run groups are few. Very often the only groupwork training received is that taught on basic social work courses. Further skills are learnt through practice experience and the limited training opportunities offered through the department. Problems may arise because workers come to groupwork with different orientations. Some will be more inclined to therapeutic approaches, perhaps because of their involvement with family therapy, while others will have more of an educational understanding (for example, they may have been involved with youth work or community work).

As mentioned previously, the emphasis on statutory work and managing a duty system often means that social workers are not given the option to use groupwork; however, this is not necessarily the case in all social work settings. In residential work, and in day centres and family centres there is, arguably, some scope for developing groupwork and educative approaches (see, for example, Brown and Clough, 1989). This may be the result of the lower priority placed on individual work in some settings, and the presence in some situations of workers from other traditions (such as youth and community work). We feel that the potential it offers as a means of educating is often denied because of this. Workers are expected to monitor the care of children within the home and rehabilitate children with their families. There may be a time when we are asked before a court to present evidence on a case. Workers are then expected by magistrates and judges to have visited the home, seen children within it and even seen a child's bedroom. This is the reality of what we do. Although we are aware of the great potential for preventive work we still tend to settle for squeezing in groupwork where we can.

Groupwork projects undertaken in social services departments are often complementary to individual casework with clients. We are not, as yet, in a position to encourage self-help groups or more structured groups for people in the community with whom we have no long-term or direct contact. Working in an area team with a small and densely populated community often lends itself to using groups as an effective means of working with people (for example, preventive groupwork with young offenders or a group for young mothers). Open-ended social groupwork projects are instigated by community workers in the area and have been very successful in enabling people to exert some control over their lives.

From the referrals at our area office, single women with children were identified as a vulnerable group. There was, or had been, a high level of statutory involvement with these women, the emphasis being on child protection. We felt that the traditional casework approach had perhaps failed to meet the complex difficulties faced by this group of women in the community. They were also a group who had no involvement with any type of community organization within the area. We judged that the woman needed to mobilize their own strengths to counteract the constant demands on their time, energy and emotional resources. Further demands were also being placed on them by us as social workers in questioning their abilities as parents.

We believe that groupwork was (and is) an appropriate way of working with single women with children. As educators, we felt that working in groups can be influential in challenging behaviour, beliefs and values, and that women learning from each other would be less threatening. We were also in agreement that the process of empowering was more effective when offered to a group.

During the first few group meetings we were able to discuss different subject areas in a light-hearted way. We talked and laughed about stereotypical roles, such as the typical social worker, teacher and health visitor. We acknowledged and challenged the women's views. The group was also able to discuss in a non-threatening way the subject of registration and the various categories of risk. We were able to clarify some of the issues surrounding registration and ask the women what they thought was the most serious form of abuse. By exchanging information between themselves and feeling safe in doing so, they could understand why their children had been registered. The women gained courage from each other by being able to ventilate and then explore their feelings of anger, frustration and unhappiness within a safe, supportive environment. They also began to understand the part that various agencies played in their lives, therefore enabling them to take some control and be self-determined.

Attendance was voluntary. The emphasis within the group meeting was on informality to ensure that the women felt comfortable enough to be able to discuss personal issues in their own lives. It was a closed group and most of the eight women attended every session, choosing to come, rather than having to be persuaded. There was always concern from the women if someone was absent and they took on the responsibility at their own instigation to contact her.

The women learnt to trust and the process of trusting each other. One woman was able to share her own experiences of being abused and later talk more about the abuse of her daughter. Other women in the group had similar experiences which they shared. The women became confident and were able to articulate their views and feelings, to be kind and caring and to listen and value each other's experiences. Some sessions were heated and emotionally charged, and it took several sessions to reach understanding and any form of agreement. We saw this as part of the learning process for the women and ourselves. By giving the women the space to think and talk about their own abusive experiences and their own needs, in turn they were able to have some insight into the needs and vulnerability of their children.

The leadership style adopted was democratic and, as group leaders, we sought to involve all members in contributing to the welfare and development of other individuals in the group. As group leaders, we facilitated working in co-operation to create a stronger interpersonal bond between members. We hoped to enable the group to complete the tasks set in a way which involved all members in group development, decision-making and action. Our style of leadership was initially direc-tive, but changed as group cohesiveness and identity developed. With skills and experience of working with women who had suffered from abuse, we had the knowledge to facilitate the group. Also as case-workers we could nurture the women and ask the right questions. Using a range of skills which we drew from psychodynamic, psychotherapeu-tic and problem-solving models we were able to move from a casework approach to an educational one and back again by using our groupwork skills.

As workers, we were able to accept some of the criticism of statutory work and question social work practice without being defensive. This was made easier for us in a group situation because of ground rules that had been set at the beginning (i.e., that information was confidential to the group). As individual social workers we are vulnerable and are often confronted because of anger and frustration at the system as a whole. We learnt from the women and welcomed their suggestions as to how, as social workers, we could work with families. The women were also able to pass on their experiences and recommendations to a person carrying out research into participation in case conferences.

The group provided a forum to combine education and self-support. The women were able to offer each other mutual support and advice. They confronted each other on issues of responsibility, particularly in child-care matters, in a more challenging way than they allowed us to do as social workers within traditional casework. Challenging us became particularly evident when talking about registration categories. They confronted each other's perceptions about abuse: one woman felt that emotional abuse was the most serious because you did not always know it was happening. There then followed a discussion about what consti-tuted emotional abuse.

A good example of the way the women learnt from their own and each other's experiences occurred when one woman's child, who was in foster care, disclosed that she had been abused. The woman was extremely upset and angry but attended the session where she was able to share her anger with the rest of the group. The women gave the mother time to talk and listened to her. One group member admitted she had suffered similar abuse. At a later session, both said that knowledge of each other's experiences had made it easier for them to talk and learn about themselves. The mother of the abused child said that having experienced the support of the group she had been better able to support her daughter.

Difficulties/restrictions on educating in social work

The difficulties of working with an educational focus should be fully recognized. In addition, as Jeffs and Smith (1990, pp. 20–1) argue, working in this way involves switching between different frames of reference; it involves the ability to draw on different understandings of our role and to carry that through in the situation. The pressure to be reactive is built into the social work response. To be proactive is working against the odds. For example, initial interaction with families is often from a referral by another agency. This triggers a number of checks in the form of the authority's child protection procedures to be carried out by the social worker. These may culminate in a visit to a home or school to see a child. Time is limited as this is done as part of a duty task, so information has to be gathered quickly to allow an assessment of the situation to be made. The referral comes through the duty system whereby each worker undertakes all tasks coming into the office for two days in every three weeks, in addition to individual caseloads. The outcome may be a decision to place the child's name on the child protection register, if the child is thought to be at risk, in order to prioritize this child's needs in the eyes of professionals. It is our experience that this response stigmatizes and sets up further stresses in families where there are already difficulties.

We have found that by working with parents, whose children have been registered, in a group setting, some of the ambiguities of the process can be addressed. For example, one woman who attended a group had been given a contract by her social worker. The expectations of the contract were that she would become involved in intensive critical work based on the level of care that she gave as a parent. Her first reaction was to become angry and dismissive. This did not surprise us as the contract had been drawn up by a social worker with whom she had had little contact. We took the opportunity at one of the group sessions to look at and discuss the contract. The initial response from the other women was to tell the social worker to mind his own business. There followed an angry debate about the uselessness of social workers. The woman told the group that she had taken the contract to her solicitor. She also said that she would refuse to work with the contract. The social worker had apparently said that her children were likely to be taken from her if she failed to co-operate. We encouraged the group to express their views. The woman was able to see that there were other points of view and that she could play the most important role by becoming involved in the process.

Although the women agreed with the inflammatory nature of the contract, they were objective and made suggestions which would ensure that she was central to the plan proposed for her children. One group member said that the woman should arrange to see her social worker and insist that the contract be discussed in detail. Another astute member suggested that the woman ask the social worker 'on what grounds' her children would be removed!

To be a social worker involves conflict with other agencies, the media and the community. This can be explained in some way by the multiple realities in which each exists and the continued belief that we are philanthropic. It is questionable whether this arises because of lack of understanding as to what we are able to do; could it sometimes be that there is no other source to which to dispatch families in need?

Alongside the limits on time and resources, we have to accommodate each worker's own beliefs and value system. In our experience the fundamental tool in statutory social work is respect for the families we are involved with. We then try to develop a dialogue, since we see this as a the basis of informal education. At the very least, undertaking work from an educational perspective encourages workers to develop a thorough understanding of the situation. The goals may not always be clear, but we try to work in a deliberate way towards an exchange of ideas and knowledge in all areas of work.

Even at the investigative stage of enquiries, we work towards conducting interviews with families in an atmosphere where both parents and workers are involved in the exchange. This takes confidence, skills and commitment to making connections with people. It is our view that this can be done, even in circumstances where families can feel threatened and defensive, be it casework, groupwork or a crisis situation. In this way, we believe being an educator in fieldwork is a way of thinking and being, rather than following a set of principles and methods which are often limited by our expectations.

In our area of social work there are often no great achievements to be made, but it may be that by chipping away at problems at all levels we can anticipate change for future generations. This often involves making fine assessments of risks, and can mean a long period of 'parenting' the parents until a point of change is reached.

Working relationships with families often become suspended during court proceedings. It is not unusual to have been working with families for many months under very difficult circumstances leading to a court hearing, and then to find that in the space of a couple of hours we lose all communication. This is because of the tensions and contradictory messages often generated in the courts as professionals vie for status, each anxious to display the infallibility of their particular field. This experience can be deleterious to families, causing unbridgeable gaps in working together.

The pressures can overwhelm the best of workers. It leads to defensive practice and a view that in order to make sense of what we do, child protection requires only refined skills in the areas of monitoring, administration and assessment. The tensions of working in statutory work are increasing as local government moves towards local budgeting and statutory reform as in the 1989 Children Act with its huge resource implications. Authorities are likely to see education as residual in terms of practice priorities.

Given that we believe that poverty denies access to education of all kinds, learning opportunities for the majority of those we are working with are severely limited. We find that children with difficulties are often non-school attenders or have been expelled because schools cannot cope with their disruptive behaviour. These children often have parents who have had no schooling themselves or who have suffered as a result of institutionalized care in their childhood. Such families often have little experience of how families function, and are sometimes criticized by neighbours and isolated from the community because of their unusual life style. In our experience these parents want at all costs to avoid their children being accommodated by the local authority, and want to care for them, but often have difficulty meeting their own needs. We work daily with families whose day-to-day existence is a struggle to provide food and fend off pressures from social workers, schools and health visitors, and whose anxieties inhibit the family's ability to function even further. This obviously creates barriers to working in an educative way and constructive involvement to the point that families have eventually fewer roads to go down. Care may become the only real option, when all coping abilities have been exhausted.

Being an educator might in the future be acknowledged as being a social work task in the same way as identifying children at risk; undertaking therapeutic work with children; and being an advocate for children and families. An educational approach does not deny the policing role within statutory social work. In our view, it offers an increased involvement with those with whom we work and can enhance feelings of self-worth. While acknowledging many of the restrictions posed by working in an educational way, if we as social workers were to do nothing to address these the loss to practice would be great, as it offers a way of generating change.

Conclusion

We have discussed education as an emerging dimension of more established practice. While it might seem to be moving in the realms of fantasy, we suggest it is necessary at this stage to look at the alternatives to embracing educating as a practice method. Can we afford to continue to deny the powerlessness and poverty which most of our clients live with? In moving towards a practice which enables people to take control, we begin to play a part on the stage. We have found there are definite gains to be made in terms of the release of energy and self-esteem, whilst offering a way of working which is stimulating and rewarding in an area of social work which otherwise raises a minefield of self-doubt. Social workers often ask themselves why they became social workers: 'What happened to the desire to help?' Social work training does not equip us to be educators.

The target may be a long way off, but this process begins with where the individuals are at. It can be used with anyone engaged with the family: home-care workers, health workers, residential care staff and foster carers. Given that the major theme expressed in the 1989 Children Act is one of partnership with parents and the sharing of parental responsibility, maintaining good relationships with parents and good quality contact between them and children calls for professional skills and other resources. A key strand in this must be educational practice. However, we do need to appreciate that this is, to some extent, a British experience. Some European approaches to social work do appear to involve an explicit educative dimension, such as the focus on social pedagogy in Germany or the concern with animation in France (see Cannan, Berry and Lyons, 1992). The challenge for us is to accommodate this in a complementary way with more familiar therapeutic and policing approaches.

Questions for consideration

1   What response would you give to a family who daily visited the office to see you, often requesting money? This is a family whose

outgoings exceed its income and which is often left short of food at the end of the week. (This needs to be discussed in the context of an educational approach.)

2 You have been asked to set up a group for young women leaving local authority care: (a) What would your aims and objectives be? (b) How would you 'educate' within the group informally and formally?

3 Why are children's names placed on the child protection register? Does anyone benefit from this? How would you work in an educative way in that context?

4 Social workers work within a multi-disciplinary setting. Can you foresee any difficulties arising when working in an educative way?

5 A holistic approach to social work involves moving between different frames of reference. At one moment workers have to police a situation, at another they may draw on therapeutic insights or act as educator. Are you comfortable with making these sorts of movement? How can you improve your abilities in this area?

References

Brown, A. and R. Clough (eds) (1989) *Groups and Grouping. Life and Work in Day and Residential Centres.* London: Routledge.

Cannan, C., L. Berry and K. Lyons (1992) *Social Work and Europe.* London: Macmillan.

Gertig, P. (1990) 'Working with carers', in T. Jeffs and M. Smith (eds), *Using Informal Education. An Alternative to Casework, Teaching and Control.* Milton Keynes: Open University Press.

Jeffs, T. and M. Smith (1990) (eds) *Using Informal Education. An Alternative to Casework, Teaching and Control.* Milton Keynes: Open University Press.

Mullender, A. and D. Ward (1991) *Self Directed Groupwork. Users Take Action for Empowerment.* London: Whiting & Birch.

Rogers, C. (1983) *Freedom to Learn in the '80s.* Ohio: Charles Merrill.

9

Supervising

MARY TURNER

From the onset of training social workers are obliged to submit themselves to supervision. The reasons for this are often poorly explained. As a consequence the grasp of what supervision means and entails, as well as its underlying purpose, can remain vague. The paradox is that there are few other professions where supervision is as highly valued and revered. Most social workers continue to demand supervision long after the completion of their training. Despite this positive culture many experiences of supervision disappoint and frustrate. This contrast between the real and the hoped for is often recounted by social workers. Why is this so? One possible explanation is that dissatisfaction is a by-product of the privacy that envelops supervisory relationships and which inhibits collective analysis and evaluation. A second is that, like the role of the college tutor, the function and purpose of supervisor has attracted little critical questioning and scrutiny.

By contrast with this Mary Turner has thought carefully about the role of supervision in professional practice. Through analyzing both her own and others' experiences she is able to convey a picture of the real contribution which supervision can make to work with clients. This chapter is a very well argued example of theory-making: tacking back and forth between theory and each new piece of practice is very evident in the example she gives. Central to her understanding is the recognition that there will be parallels between the model of supervision which workers experience and the way they work with clients. Supervisors who try to control their supervisees, or encourage their dependency, are likely to find that their workers repeat this pattern with clients. Many of us will recognize this pattern, whilst others will take a different view of how these sets of relationships influence one another.

Like Walker and Marshall she acknowledges that social workers often deny uneasy or unacceptable feelings of doubt and uncertainty. She shows how supervisors need to avoid collusion with workers if they are to enable them to recognize and deal with these feelings. This kind of collusion can occur, for example, if a supervisor becomes simply a supportive friend to the supervisee. Earlier chapters have emphasized the need for workers to be honest with themselves. Mary Turner recognizes the role which supervisors can play in this process through encouraging workers to be thoughtful about their feelings regarding their work. Drawing upon her own practice she reveals the myriad ways in which supervisors may enable workers to look beneath the surface of their own experiences.

Many readers will be particularly interested in her discussion about whether and how managers can use supervision. Her emphasis in this, as in other supervisory relationships, is on the necessity of enabling workers to develop autonomy rather than dependence. Mary's example shows that supervisors, too, have needs, and that they will continue to have uncomfortable feelings. Confronting the tendency which many of us have to want to rescue and/or control others is not something which is ever finally overcome. It is possible, though, for supervisors to some extent to supervise themselves and hence have a way of dealing with these dangers. Many of us will find it useful to think about, and discuss, the question of how we can ensure that we continue to supervise effectively.

* * *

Workers and supervisors are sometimes confused by the word 'supervision' as it is commonly used in social work and related professions. It is a term which can trigger thoughts and feelings about being watched critically at work by someone in authority, or of being corrected or controlled. I hope to show that professional supervision is something different.

I find it helpful to think of supervision as 'super vision': 'super' in this sense suggests that the supervisor can have a larger and freer view of the work the worker describes to them simply because they are not directly embroiled in it. The worker is involved in the work, both intellectually and emotionally, and this makes it more difficult for him or her to think objectively about it. By listening carefully, questioning and exploring the worker's perceptions of his or her own work, the supervisor helps the worker to see more parts of the pattern, and the worker's own role within it, than would otherwise be likely.

From an ethical standpoint it is important that those working intimately with the public should bring their work regularly to supervision. There is a danger otherwise that the worker may fall into unprofessional – or just plain unhelpful and ineffective – practice. Kitto and Christian (1987, p. 1) note that the origins of supervision as a professional practice lie in the psychoanalytic movement. Here there was a need to train and support therapists who were doing difficult, confidential work with clients, usually alone. Anyone working with clients in disturbed and emotionally charged situations is vulnerable to taking into themselves considerable confusion and chaos. Consequently, it becomes difficult for workers to hold on to their capacity to think clearly and independently about their work.

Supervision aims to enable workers to hold on to this kind of thinking capacity. Through thinking better, they are likely to deal more effectively with the confusion and anxiety inherent in their work. They will be freer to evaluate their role and, as a result, will work better with their clients. Social workers are under additional pressure in many cases to achieve more with less resources. The temptation for them is to rush around 'doing things', in an effort to satisfy the demands and relieve their own anxiety, and it becomes even more difficult for them to safeguard thinking time. A good supervisor helps workers to keep the aims of their work in focus, so that they are better able to prioritize and evaluate what they do.

Managing anxiety and confusion

It is important to the development of the professional worker that they are helped to acknowledge, understand and manage areas of anxiety and confusion. An important function of supervision is to enable this to happen by creating a culture where this is seen as acceptable and useful. Many workers feel they must appear to be coping well with their work at all times. What they see as their less acceptable thoughts, feelings and actions are suppressed, denied and avoided, for fear of being seen as not a good-enough worker. It is important for supervisors to demonstrate in supervision their own capacity to contain anxiety and remain thoughtful about whatever the worker brings, rather than avoiding the painful issues, rushing for solutions, or giving 'neat' packages of instructions. If this happens the worker will be enabled gradually to do this for him- or herself: 'to internalize a thinking person' (Salzberger-Wittenberg, Henry and Osborne, 1983, p. 60).

Supervision provides a framework within which workers are helped to sort out the nature of their work experiences and give them meaning. In doing so, confusion and anxiety is modulated and the workers' internal world of thoughts and feelings becomes more manageable and stable. This process, of course, reflects precisely the kind of help which social workers in turn need to be able to provide for their clients. They are more likely to be able to do so if they have experienced it themselves.

If supervisors are to enable these kinds of processes to happen through supervision, it follows that they too will need to acknowledge and manage their own confusion, uncertainties and anxieties. If they do not, they will not be able to tolerate these things in the worker and, therefore, will be unable to help them. The higher up the professional ladder we get, the harder it often becomes to acknowledge our own confusion, anxiety and uncertainty. We fear that if we do, we will be seen by our colleagues as less competent.

Whose perceptions?

An important principle of supervision is that it is the worker's own perceptions which form the focus of the session. Supervisors often find this a difficult boundary to hold, especially if they are also the worker's manager or student's placement manager. As they are then likely to actually see the worker at work, they might also have their own view of the events that the worker describes to them in supervision, and it will probably be different from the worker's. It is tempting for supervisors to make their own perception of the work the focus, giving the worker their own judgments upon it. This defeats the purpose of supervision.

Supervision should help workers to become more able to take responsibility for their own work – thoughts, feelings and actions – and to make better judgments about it for themselves. The ability to do this is at the heart of working professionally. It is, after all, the workers (and not the supervisors) who have to go back and work with the client or situation. They will not be able to do so effectively if they are dependent upon their supervisor to evaluate their work and make judgments about it for them. All they can then do is keep coming back to their supervisor for 'more'.

The manager as supervisor

We have seen that it is often more difficult for managers supervising their own workers to keep the focus of supervision on the worker's perceptions of his or her work rather than on their own. Attempts have been made to get around this difficulty by creating a distinction between 'managerial' and 'non-managerial' supervision, and there seems to be a lot of confusion about what the differences are. I suggest that the aims and processes of supervision should be the same whoever is doing the supervising, and that 'managerial supervision' should simply mean a manager using supervision as one way of developing staff.

Supervision is an effective tool for professional staff development which managers would be foolish not to consider. However, many managers subvert the supervision process into a means of controlling or instructing staff, instead of a means of developing staff. It is not difficult to understand why this happens. The manager is, after all, ultimately responsible for the work of the agency, and is more emotionally and intellectually involved in the worker's work than an 'outside' supervisor may be. This can create anxiety for the manager/supervisor and make it difficult for him or her to allow members of staff the freedom to create their own 'agenda' for supervision.

Managers can never escape from the fact that they are ultimately responsible, but they do need to ask themselves:

- 'What kind of professional workers do I want?'
- 'What kind of professional workers do I need in order that the work of the agency may be done effectively?'

In social work, the answer to the second question is undoubtedly that they need workers who can take responsibility for their own work; who can think deeply and independently about it; and who can assess and make judgments about their own performance. Dependent workers who can only follow instructions and rely on their managers to make judgments for them will never work really effectively with clients.

The answer to the first question, 'What kind of professional workers do I want?' may be rather different. Many managers – although they would probably not care to admit it – would actually prefer their professional staff to be non-autonomous people who follow instructions rather than thinking for themselves. They are perceived as less of a threat to the manager's authority.

Workers, too, are often ambivalent about taking responsibility for their own work. Even those workers who complain most vociferously about managerial constraints upon them are often, themselves, afraid of exercising their autonomy. It is easy for managers and workers to collude in this to avoid their mutual anxieties. Managers manage in a constraining, controlling way which inhibits professional development, but which makes them feel safer. Workers go along with this and, whilst they complain about the constraints upon them, they have the comfort of knowing that they will not have to take responsibility for their own work.

One of the first principles of management, according to Drucker (1977) is to make the worker 'achieving'. We have already seen what qualities social workers must have if they are to achieve. Managers who hang on to control of their workers, using supervision merely as a forum to put across their own views, will not develop staff who can work in this way. Supervision can be used as part of an overall approach to managing professional people which encourages autonomy and responsibility.

Looking beneath the surface

A wise supervisor pays close attention not only to what workers talk about in supervision, but also to why they may have chosen this particular aspect of their work, and the way in which they present it in the session. Often this will indicate something of what is going on – perhaps at a less consciously acknowledged level – in the relationship between workers and their clients. It may reflect not only the difficulties which a client has, but also unresolved conflicts in a worker.

If supervisors are alert to this possibility, they then have the opportunity to work with the workers on those conflicts which have been activated in them by their encounter with the client, and which are probably blocking the work. Workers often present such blockages in supervision as the client's problem, but the supervisor will understand that: 'the [workers] will select from their interventions with the client some area of conflict in which they unconsciously merge with the client and will present this material for the supervisor to "cure"' (Alonso, 1985, p. 122). Consequently, as they listen to the worker, supervisors will be wondering, 'Why is the supervisee telling me this and in this particular way?'

Example

Carol is a residential social worker in a unit for adolescent girls. The unit is shortly to close and the girls are to be relocated to various other units around the large rural county council area. This will mean splitting up a small group of girls with whom Carol has worked closely for some time.

In supervision Carol said she thought the girls were upset and anxious about the closing down of the unit and would miss each other and the staff. She knew that she needed to help the girls to deal with the closure but said that they did not seem to want to talk about it. She felt the girls were embarrassed to show sad feelings in front of their friends and were avoiding the issue by displaying a 'don't care' attitude.

The supervisor noticed that Carol had not spoken of her own feelings about the closure, although it meant change and loss for her too. The supervisor also recalled another occasion when Carol told him how afraid she felt of being seen (and seeing herself) as weak, emotional and unable to cope.

The supervisor asked Carol what she felt about losing the unit and her group of girls. With encouragement she was able to express her own sadness, anger, sense of loss and worries about her future. She recalled some of the good and bad times she and the girls had experienced together, and what she had learnt from being with them. As they explored this, and her fear of being unable to cope in an emotional situation, Carol saw that she had been attributing all the avoidance of facing up to the ending to the group and not seeing her own reluctance to face it.

As Carol found that it was possible in supervision to acknowledge and work on her own thoughts and feelings about the ending, so she became more confident in thinking about how she might enable the girls to do the same.

This example shows how important it is for supervisors to help workers focus on underlying aspects of themselves which may be affecting the work. In this case, the clues were provided by the parallels which the supervisor noticed between the perceived blocks for the clients and for the worker, and the way the worker presented this to the supervisor.

Often supervision in social work and other settings will tend to focus solely upon what the worker has done and what they need to do next. It is understandable that both supervisor and worker might prefer to focus on actions, or planning actions, because this is easier to look at (being both more tangible and less unsettling) than what may be underlying the worker's actions. Looking at the worker's actions is, however, a very good place to start in supervision: 'Tell me what you did ...'. But if supervisors stop there, or go enthusiastically into planning what the worker might do next, they leave untouched the key to understanding the way the worker works. They ignore the processes underlying the actions and how these are influenced by the worker's own attitudes, values, beliefs, assumptions, etc. Until workers understand something of this, it is difficult for them to change in ways which enable them to work more effectively with their clients.

The experience of supervision

In an ideal situation, workers come to supervision bringing a piece of their work to explore with the supervisor. The supervisor enables workers to examine their perceptions of it and understand it more fully, especially their own functioning within it. Workers then leave with a clearer view of themselves and their work and, as a natural consequence of this, are in a better position to see how to take the work forward. However, because supervision takes place in the context of a relationship between the supervisor and the worker, where there are two people's needs and perceptions involved, this ideal process can all too easily become distorted.

Often difficulties arise because of 'the supervisor's need to be loved admired, trusted, and remembered with affection [by the worker]' (Alonso, 1985, p. 86). These desires are natural enough in all of us but, unless recognized and managed, they can prevent the supervisor from supervising effectively: for example, they may cause supervisors to come out of their legitimate role and become a friend, or an expert to be looked up to and advised by.

Example

Jack was an enthusiastic new supervisor at a placement for a social work student. In the supervision sessions, Jack found himself becoming increasingly frustrated because the student seemed to have no curiosity about her work. She tended to wait passively in the supervision sessions for Jack to introduce something, or else she brought material about which she seemed to have no questions or concerns. Jack felt she handed this material to him to 'do' something with. He responded by working madly on the material, generating all kinds of questions and theories about the work which the student accepted.

Since Jack was the placement manager and also saw the student at work, he fed in suggestions about how she might work better, which she again accepted.

Jack talked about these difficulties at a supervisors' training group. The group helped him realize how anxious he felt that this student should do well, and how he felt that this would reflect on his own competence as a supervisor. Jack saw that he was being curious and thoughtful 'for' the student, thus confirming her in a dependent, non-thoughtful role.

Having identified his own anxieties and how they were interfering with the work, and having reclarified the task of supervision, Jack was able to change his way of working with the student. Instead of anxiously scrabbling for material to work on in the supervision sessions, or introducing material of his own from his experience of the student working in his unit, he was able to wait and tolerate some silence. He was able to ask the student how she felt in the supervision situation and focus on her difficulty in using it, and her fear of being seen as not good enough in the supervisor's eyes. As Jack managed his anxiety about his own performance, she became less dependent on him to do the thinking, and began to produce her own material for the supervision sessions.

This example shows the two sets of needs and perceptions which were operating in the relationship and the result. In this case the anxieties of both parties were preventing the real work of supervision from being done. As a result of his anxiety about being a good supervisor, Jack had allowed himself to come out of role, encouraged by the student's passive dependency, which was her way of coping with her own anxiety about the supervision. Once the supervisor had acknowledged and begun to manage his own anxiety, he could help the student worker to do the same.

Being supportive

The example of Jack shows how, because of his own anxiety, he was attempting to rescue the worker from her difficulties by doing her thinking for her. The desire to rescue is common in 'the caring professions', causing workers to keep their clients dependent upon them rather than fostering their autonomy.

Supervisors may rescue workers in a variety of ways, rather than helping them to take responsibility for their own work. For example, they may do the thinking for the worker (as Jack did), or provide solutions or instructions. In the case of students, supervisors may give a more favourable assessment to the training agency than is accurate, so that the student will not fail. This type of supervisor behaviour is often described as 'being supportive' to the worker, but it is actually the opposite. True support comes from a supervisor who can help workers to acknowledge, understand and work on their difficulties.

Building trust

The supervisor's need to be 'loved, trusted and remembered with affection' (Alonso, 1985, p. 86) can lead to a blurring of the boundary of the supervisory relationship so that it becomes a friendly, social relationship instead. Supervisors may worry that the worker will see them as cold and clinical. Workers may fear supervisor criticism or feel that they need to 'get to know' the supervisor before they can trust them enough to work with them. And so both parties collude to avoid their anxieties by developing a friendly, social kind of relationship. The end result is that supervision becomes no more than a friendly chat about 'how the work is going', lacking any edge or rigour.

Often the reasoning behind this kind of supervisory behaviour is that the supervisor and the worker will work better together if they trust and feel more comfortable with each other. This reasoning is a misunderstanding of the nature of relationships and the building of trust. Most working relationships must begin with some mutual doubt and discomfort. It is as we risk ourselves in working together that we prove ourselves to be trustworthy or not, and our trust and confidence in each other either grows or diminishes.

Control

The issue of control in the supervisory relationship often creates anxiety for both parties. Supervisors may worry that if they do not control the supervision they will be seen as weak, or perhaps that they will be unable to cope with what the worker brings. Supervisor control can take a number of forms: for example, taking charge of the agenda for the session or telling the worker how to work with particular clients.

Some supervisors are at a stage in their professional life when their role brings them little face-to-face client contact. Working on the worker's clients 'through' supervision may fulfil a wish in them to feel in contact with clients. The temptation for the supervisor in this situation is to try to get the worker to work with the clients as they themselves would have done.

The result of a controlling supervisor can be either compliant workers, or workers who battle for control themselves, fearing that if they do not control the supervisor then the supervisor will control them. Competitiveness and envy are common in this kind of supervisory relationship, and this is usually underpinned by feelings of insecurity in both parties.

The development of the supervisory relationship

Like any relationship, a supervisory one changes and develops over time. The following example charts the changing processes of a supervisory relationship between Ann, a student social worker, and her supervisor during her course.

Example

At the beginning of the supervisory relationship, Ann felt anxious about what it would entail. She had not been in formal education since leaving school and the model she expected from supervision was similar to that of the teacher/pupil relationships she had known. Much of her anxiety was related to this model. Would the supervisor approve or disapprove of her? Would she be expected to have the 'right' answers? Would she be criticized and made to feel small? Coupled with this were dependency feelings: 'The supervisor will tell me what to do and where I am going wrong.'

Ann was late for her first supervision sessions. She arrived hot, anxious and defensive, expecting the supervisor either to be annoyed with her, as her teachers might have been, or to be sympathetic and tell her it was all right. She was surprised when the supervisor made little comment and, without blame or rancour, began the session. Ann was surprised again, and rather angry, when the supervisor did not offer to give her any extra time to make up for her lateness. Ann felt that this was uncaring of the supervisor.

Later in the supervisory relationship, Ann realized that the supervisor was not uncaring but was simply treating her as an adult, responsible for herself, rather than as a child. This helped Ann to understand that it was possible for her to hold her own boundaries of time, task and role too (as the supervisor had done). This was something Ann found difficult to do with clients and in her life in general. She tended to be 'all over the place', not managing her time, taking on too much, trying to be everything to everyone, yet often feeling confused, resentful and ineffective.

The supervisor felt anxious when the student was late: maybe the student did not want to work with her, or was not finding their sessions useful. She also felt irritated at having to put time aside for Ann. She had to remind herself that this was the student's time – no more and no less – and that all she need do was to stay within her supervisor role as best she could.

The early stages of supervision were also marked for Ann by ambivalent feelings about the supervisor. On one hand, she tended to idealize the supervisor and have an unrealistic view of her insight and knowledge. On the other hand, this made Ann feel vulnerable, as though the supervisor could 'see' even the things she did not want to reveal. She also felt quite dependent and wanted, for her own security, to keep her view of the supervisor as the one who 'knew'.

It was rather flattering for the supervisor to feel held by Ann in such a position of wisdom and omniscience, and she needed to remind herself of her real capacities and limitations. She could only know of Ann what Ann allowed her to see, and she knew that it was her job to help Ann find her own insights rather than rely on the supervisor's. Ann sometimes felt angry and confused because the supervisor was not fitting in with her preconceptions of how their relationship should be, and based largely on her experiences at school. It was as though Ann was transferring her mental and emotional 'map' from the teacher/pupil relationships on to this new relationship. It took Ann some time to gradually update her 'map' and revise her view of supervision and of herself in relation to it. One of the things that enabled her to do this was that the supervisor did not play into the anticipated role but treated the student as an adult.

As they moved into the middle stages of their work together, Ann's new 'map' came more fully into operation. Once Ann discovered that supervision was useful, she gradually risked bringing more of her deeper anxieties, doubts and confusion about her work for exploration. She stopped trying to impress the supervisor and brought material that she really needed to understand better.

There was still a level of dependency upon the supervisor. For example, when problems arose between supervision sessions, Ann would mentally put them on one side to take to the supervisor, not feeling confident to think them through by herself.

As they moved into the ending phase of the supervisory relationship, the supervisor noticed that this was changing. Ann was more independent. She was thinking through problems for herself as they arose – or making use of other resources – without needing to wait for supervision. Ann said that she felt she often 'supervised herself' now, as though she had internalized the supervision process. She was more able to take what she needed from supervision rather than feel dependent on it.

The supervisor felt some pangs because Ann did not now need her as she had done before. She reminded herself that this was as it should be, and resisted a wish to hold on to Ann. She encouraged her independence.

In conclusion

This is an example of the developing processes in one supervisory relationship, but there are themes within it that have more general applicability. They crop up frequently. It shows the need for the worker to develop greater autonomy, and how old perceptions and ways of relating can be transferred to the supervisory relationship. These are often related to teacher/pupil or parent/child relationships. The ways in which the supervisor held her own role and its proper boundaries, by managing her own needs and anxieties, provided both a model and a framework for the worker to update her perceptions and behaviour. It shows that for most worker anxieties about supervision, there is a corresponding supervisor anxiety. These are the traps into which the supervisor can fall, hindering opportunities for the worker's development. This emphasizes the need for supervisors to be constantly vigilant in monitoring their own emotional responses to the worker they are supervising.

A great deal has been said and written in social work and related professions about 'enabling' and 'empowering' clients, but it seems that much actual practice does not reflect this, and that a dependency model is still common. Supervision is one way of enabling greater autonomy in social workers themselves. The chances are that they will then be better able to help their clients towards greater autonomy too.

Questions for consideration

1 What images and feelings does the word 'supervision' conjure up for you?
2 Can you identify where these images and feelings may have come from?
3 If you have experienced being supervised, what were for you: (a) the main benefits; (b) the main frustrations; (c) the main anxieties?
4 As a supervisee what do you have to do to maximize the potential of supervision?
5 In what ways do you think good supervision can be supportive?

References

Alonso, A. (1985) *The Quiet Profession.* London: Macmillan.
Drucker, P. (1977) *People and Performance.* London: Heinemann.
Kitto, J. and C. Christian (1987) *The Theory and Practice of Supervision.* London: Centre for Professional Studies in Informal Education, YMCA National College.
Salzberger-Wittenberg, I., G. Henry and E. Osborne (1983) *The Emotional Experience of Learning and Teaching.* London: Routledge & Kegan Paul.

10

Managing

JENNIFER LAPOMPE

Few areas of practice have received more attention in recent years than that of the management of social work. Literature and training courses have provided a welter of material designed largely to inform the thinking of actual or aspiring managers. Much of it is based on a crude lifting of ideas, concepts and models from industrial and commercial settings. Rarely does it inform practitioners of the realities of how they might interact with their own managers. The literature is overwhelmingly prescriptive and top-down. The language often inappropriate, whilst the intellectual base is somewhat porous. As a consequence those who enter social work management often appear ill-prepared and uncertain of touch, whilst those who are managed often possess unrealistic expectations of what could be achieved by their 'ideal manager'.

In contrast to this dominant prescriptive literature, Jennifer Lapompe engages with the real experiences of managers and those they manage. Through interviews with colleagues, both managers and managed, she is able to provide an insight into their thoughts and feelings. Jennifer shows that, just as there is a process of becoming professional whereby new social workers have to think through what professionalism means for them, a similar process is necessary for those who become managers. This frequently involves feelings of doubt and inadequacy akin to those described by Jeremy Walker. One aspect of this is thinking afresh about the relationships between one's professional self and one's private self. Jennifer shows that this is often particularly problematic for those who wish actively to reject the rather distant image which even the word 'manager' can suggest. This image is not only distant, it is also male, white, heterosexual and able-bodied. Those who are committed to anti-oppressive practice will face particular challenges in forming a comfortable identity whilst allowing themselves to be, at times, less than perfect.

A key aspect of challenging some of our received models of management is through ensuring that management preserves and encourages the autonomy of workers. Jenny extends this possibility through looking critically at management from the point of view of those who are managed, and provides a set of their expectations drawn from her interviews. Her aim is to encourage workers to define their own management needs in the workplace.

Some of us will perhaps be surprised at the fact that that the workers who are quoted in this chapter often have negative things to say about management. Undoubtedly conscientious managers will strive to do better after reading these comments. However, there are deeper points to think about here. These involve the necessity for each of us to confront and explore the origins of our ideas about management and to consider appropriate roles for managers in relation to autonomous practice.

* * *

For me, managing conjures up a picture of someone with outstretched, elongated arms trying to hold everything together in an attempt to nurture, encourage, motivate, produce and deliver. The reality is more of an octopus with eight arms trying to juggle or balance all the elements involved in managing a service.

What do we mean by 'managing'? Does the task carried out by managers or the things they think they should be doing mirror or reflect the views of the staff they manage, or the people they provide a service for? Do the ideals about managing reflect the reality of what they actually do? In this chapter I will explore my experience and that of other managers within social work, identifying the tasks and some of the constraints.

For this chapter I have asked people why they wanted to be managers. How much can they be themselves in their role as managers, or do they have to become some other 'being' to do the job? I asked others about their expectations of those being managed. Which tasks get shelved when coping with crisis, and what gets neglected?

In an attempt to tackle these questions I have drawn on the experiences of field social workers, intermediate treatment officers and home-care organizers from a culturally diverse inner city borough which has pioneered a decentralization programme aiming to bring services to the community at a local level. Much of the content of this chapter will be based on verbatim statements made by practitioners.

Managing: what is it all about?

One practitioner describes managing as: 'ensuring services are delivered to clients within a policy framework. Ensuring resources (including staff) are used effectively and efficiently'. Others defined the task of managing variously: supporting staff, providing supervision, facilitating staff meetings; training; taking responsibility for budgets; monitoring and evaluating service delivery; public relations work (i.e., selling the service); taking responsibility for ensuring staff develop professionally and personally; liaising with other departments; developing policy and practice; sharing knowledge and expertise with staff; and 'carrying the can' when things go wrong.

Good managers carry staff with them. They should encourage them to get involved in decision-making processes, delegating responsibilities which enable staff to grow and develop. They should be able to carry out tasks confidently and effectively, as well as being able to say honestly, 'I don't know but I will find out and let you know.' Managers should allow staff to make choices and create an environment of trust. They should avoid the official 'by-the-book' approach.

You sometimes hear workers say to their managers, 'I wouldn't do your job if you paid me'; of course, there is the bigger salary and it is a good career move, but are there other reasons why managers want the job? One manager said: 'When I was a worker I thought that service delivery was poor, I wanted to improve it ... basically I thought I could do a better job than my old manager.' You often do. We quickly learn how not to do things. Another said: 'Being a manager gives me more power. I am able to give the clients more choice. I wanted to do the job the way I thought it should be done when I was a basic grade worker.'

As for me, why did I want the job? I wanted to be a manager because I thought that I might be in a better position to influence policy and practice. I wanted to be in a position where I was involved when decisions were being made, and where I could put items on the agenda when they would otherwise be excluded. I felt that as a manager I could challenge discrimination at a higher level and make demands for a service that reflected a wider range of needs, especially in relation to race and gender. I wanted the job because I knew I could develop and provide, along with the assistance of a good staff team, an efficient service to the community and to the clients.

Many of you may have good reasons for wanting to be managers. It is not always about those extra £ signs floating across your eyes, although they are very welcome.

The reality of management

You take with you good and bad experiences and you feel you can do a better job. The reality is that you get caught up in structures and procedures which are not designed to make your job as a manager easy. You often find that the things you want to do are largely influenced by external forces over which you have little or no control. There are a number of frustrations experienced by managers at all levels, and indeed by the workers. One manager expressed his concern that: 'the lack of resources and feeling of being under the threat of further cuts adds up on a day to day basis to a department that cannot hear the concerns you are trying to express, since everyone is already overstretched and then nothing gets properly dealt with'.

Any possible developments are often blocked by senior management, lack of policy, bureaucracy or financial constraints. One manager had this to add: 'managing staff means you always need to be there for somebody and you have to be strong enough for them and seen as always coping'.

I guess managers are expected to be super beings. However, I sometimes feel as though I am sticking plaster on wounds and not much more. The solutions are sometimes clear: you know what is needed to ease the plight of a particular client, but you are constrained by external forces and lack of resources. You silently collude because effectively you have become powerless. The real decision and the power lies at a political level where the motivating factors are often financial rather than welfare-orientated. Yet, within all this, as managers we somehow have to generate enthusiasm and motivation within our staff team in order to keep morale high so we can continue to provide a service in the best possible way.

I know that sometimes I want to say, 'What's it all about? What are we really doing? Do I believe in this any more?' Before getting absorbed with a discussion of crises and conflict we must remember the positives. There are small successes: you may have marginally improved someone's 'lot' or simply made them feel a little better about themselves. Although that is not enough, it provides some satisfaction. One manager said she enjoys managing and gets on well with staff.

> We are able to sit and talk to one another about anything so we have trust which is vital and never having to act like a 'boss' ... I see myself as an overseer of a service but my staff are the true value of the service, they know the job and clients inside out.

In regard to managing a crisis, clearly some tasks have to be set aside. A concern for one manager was that when dealing with a crisis there is a need for stronger management in order to keep things on an even keel, to stop things falling apart and, at the same time, to provide staff with clear directions. The manager felt that being personally involved in a crisis made it difficult to keep a cool head without seeming to be cold. One answer could be that, given the nature of the work, you cannot afford to be too emotional or attached, and somehow you need to distance yourself in order to make clear, effective decisions.

When asked about what gets neglected, most managers said things like supervision sessions, training and staff meetings. I agree entirely with this, but for me there are other things that have to be added: for example, paperwork, bills that need to be signed and processed, letters that need a response, training applications that are late. The scenario is this:

> You decide from the week before that today is going to be your quiet day, the day you would spend in the office clearing your tray. You get in, make your cup of tea and sit down ready to tackle the 'pile'. Within minutes the staff are on top of you, and whoever's not hovering over you has pulled up a chair opposite, each with a burning story about one of their clients that they need to tell you about now. Two

hours later they are still talking; you have to listen, they need to offload.

Another scenario:

The phone rings: one of your young people has been arrested. The keyworker and most of the staff are out: those who are in are occupied with clients; what can you do, since you have to deal with it?

or:

The phone rings: can you attend an urgent case conference as some child is being received into care today?

There goes that quiet day. These experiences are real ones. What makes it all worthwhile is that sometimes your efforts get recognized. One manager said that despite everything he got satisfaction from: 'the feeling that staff appreciate your efforts to support them in the work they are doing; from feedback from outside that the service provided is appreciated and valued; and from a general belief that my management is providing the most effective possible service to clients'. Another described the satisfaction as coming from: 'knowing that we do as much as we can for the users of the service'.

Another area I discussed with managers was how their personality featured and whether their ideals of managing matched with what they actually did. Managers carry with them a number of skills and qualities which are reflected in their interactions with others. One manager had this to say:

In reality I believe we all look to our own interest as workers. This can (but not always) lead to conflicts with my own ideal of trying to provide the best kind of service ... I am there to direct, support, advise, monitor and evaluate what staff are doing. I don't want to separate my personality from my role as manager, but sometimes I have to ... I want to be myself at work but in reality we all adopt different roles in and out of work.

Whilst I would agree that we do adopt different roles, these still reflect our personality. We cannot completely separate who we are from the way we do things. If you are a 'cold' person, then the way you relate will reflect that. Obviously part of your 'self' may be suppressed at work, and we may not behave the same as we do outside our work environment.

We all have images of successful leaders. These are influenced by our culture, education and experiences. These also have an impact on who we are and help to shape our personality. Our background, experiences, values and beliefs generate expectations as to how we should use a leadership position to involve others. Personality traits – such as extroversion and dominance – can manifest themselves in leadership styles. This was something that several of the workers I spoke to commented on.

If you are naturally a warm person who openly cares for others, it is likely that the way you manage is not simply about meeting your organization's aims and objectives: it is also likely to be about ensuring that people are being developed, and that workers have an opportunity to discuss personal issues which may be affecting them.

A number of managers expressed concern about the balance between being dictatorial or democratic; when does support of staff become controlling or overly interventionist? In particular, what about dealing with conflict? As one person I spoke to said: 'there is only one of me and several of them'. Staff can usually be managed in a relaxed and flexible way and this can be achieved by setting clear standards according to which you expect your staff to operate. If people know what is expected of them and structures and procedures are clear, then they can get on with their work without the 'boss' leaning over their shoulder. There may need to be the occasional reminder if things begin to slip, as they often do, but it is not necessary to become an 'alien' to carry out your task as a manager. Managers who hide behind the power that goes with the job and dictate to workers are often not very confident within that role. If managers assume a role that is contrary to, or incompatible with, their personality, it will soon be detected. A weak ineffectual character can no more become a powerful dictator than a 'Hitler' can operate in a democratic way. They may go undetected until challenged.

In terms of management styles, there is no hard or fast rule that can be applied in all circumstances. I manage within a framework which reflects my perception of good management skills and personal qualities. Managers should manage people as individuals. It is a nonsense to believe that you manage all your staff in the same way; different people require different approaches, although professional expectations may be similar.

A good manager needs to have an awareness that people respond in varied ways to different management styles. As individuals we are often at different levels of confidence and competence, and this should be recognized by managers when deciding what style of leadership to adopt. In some instances the directive, autocratic style may be more appropriate. For example, one manager I spoke to had a member of staff who, at times, was very difficult to manage. This particular staff members often ended up rowing with the manager, refusing to do the task requested. The manager found himself in a position whereby he had to instruct the person in order to get results. The manager said, however, that he usually adopted a 'democratic leader' approach whereby he involves others in dialogue and decisions. He admitted that he recognized the need to adapt his style to suit the individuals he managed.

I believe managers need to know when to use which style with which person. It is fairly easy to get it wrong and to have a negative impact. For instance, how many times have we all come across managers who always seem to be telling their best staff what to do? The staff resent it because they are competent and already know the ropes. When thinking about leadership there are various ways of categorising styles. I have found Blanchard's (1988) analysis of four common styles helpful.

1 *Directing*. This approach is for people who lack competence but who are enthusiastic and committed. They need direction and supervision to get them started.
2 *Coaching*. This style is for people who have some competence but lack commitment. They need direction and supervision, and also support and praise to build their self-esteem. The aim is to involve them in decision-making so as to restore commitment.
3 *Supporting*. People who have competence but lack confidence and motivation can be supported. They do not need much directing because they have the skills and abilities. However, support is necessary to bolster their confidence and motivation.
4 *Delegating*. Those that have both competence and commitment, who are able and willing to work by themselves with little supervision or support and can be left to get on with the work, provided that they have a clear idea of their task and understand the boundaries of their role. In a highly responsible profession such as social work, where sound judgment is vital, it is important that we nurture workers confidence and skills.

Alongside individual competence and confidence managers also need to take account of people's domestic situations, cultural needs, race, gender, sexuality, disability, and so on. All these factors have an impact on the way we relate to others, and as managers we need to be sensitive to people's needs. For example, a manager may need to acknowledge that domestic commitments, particularly responsibility for child or other forms of care, often feature more highly for female staff than males, and time off may need to be negotiated. When managing someone with a 'disability' we need to ensure that demands made on that individual are not unrealistic. At the same time we have to guard against patronizing them. Managers need to have a strong commitment to, and understanding of, equal opportunities and ensure that people's differences are acknowledged and treated with respect.

Managers are people first, and we often hold our personal prejudices. These can manifest themselves in the attitudes we take with, and the manner in which we manage, individual staff. It is important that we recognize our own prejudices and work with them.

Being managed

Managers' impressions of what they offer staff in terms of managing may not match up to the experiences of those being managed. What a manager perceives as supportive may be viewed as inhibiting or disabling by a worker. Let's look at what some workers had to say about being managed:

> Being managed means being enabled to work at one's optimum level, in one's own way and to develop one's own style of working with the full support of the accountable person ... it is necessary for managers and the person being managed to have some confidence and trust in each other and to be able to sustain this relationship over time, despite difference of opinions or approach.

Another defined it as: 'a monitoring and guiding role, ensuring that practice is following departmental policy and procedures. That statutory obligations are being met in full, that workers' time is being used appropriately ... being encouraged (actively) to develop skills, knowledge, learning and confidence through training, group supervision, etc. Another worker said that he expected to be enabled to be efficient and in control of his work: 'to be accountable for your overall functioning to your manager ... to obtain support, advice for efficiency in work and job satisfaction, to be encouraged to develop and be creative.

Let's list some of their expectations.

- To be treated like a reasonably intelligent adult
- Not to be told how to do things just because that is the way the manager would have done it
- Not to have your confidence undermined, but rather to be enabled to develop self-confidence
- To feel safe and at ease to discuss difficult issues
- To be provided with advice and support at both a practical and emotional level
- To be able to 'laugh' with or at the person who manages you

It was felt that there should be a balance between giving clear guidelines for workers and allowing workers to make their own decisions and to be autonomous.

The experience of one worker was of being guided step by step in casework. The manager made lists and ticked items off when the tasks were done: 'as I was a new worker at the time this was not terribly resented but after a couple of weeks I could do without it ... the manager stopped because I no longer took notice of the list'. The worker described the experience as both good and bad: it was good in the sense that, as a new worker in a first social work job, detailed guidance was welcomed, then taken away when it was no longer needed. However, the worker wondered whether this showed that the line manager was responsive to the changing needs of one of her staff or whether the worker's needs coincided with her way of doing things. Perhaps the latter, as other more longstanding colleagues had experienced the manager in very much the same way.

Another worker was managed by someone who was uninterested in her work. She said:

> Supervision consisted of my reporting on what I was doing and receiving no comment at all. If on the odd occasion there was comment, it was put as a directive on what to do, based on no knowledge of the case because he hadn't been listening ... his laissez-faire attitude enabled me to get on with my work in an autonomous fashion but it left me totally unsupported.

Sadly, the bad experiences seem to outweigh the good by far, although workers did have some good things to say about their managers.

I have always felt valued and supported by my line manager who has gone out of her way to help me (e.g., going to college, developing the service etc.) ... we treat each other as equals even though she is on a different grade. I can talk to her and she listens.

Another positive viewpoint came from a worker who was encouraged by the fact that her manager could be relied on in a crisis and could handle situations that she did not know how to deal with.

My experience of being managed has varied according to the confidence and competence of my manager. I say this because I feel it is important to have a clear view about the job I am paid to do, the task ahead of me and my approach to it. I have tended to enter meetings with line managers with a clear agenda. One result of this is that it has not often left much room for them to direct me. Some have welcomed this because, at one level, it has made their task easier. Others found it threatening. I had one particular manager who said I was not easy to manage and that he found me challenging. This manager often made unrealistic demands with little explanation; I therefore questioned his approach. Line management meetings were unproductive and usually involved me reporting on my work, him acknowledging it and saying 'Good', or wanting to know 'in what capacity I was involved'. This was a white worker who accused me at times of doing work he should be doing and getting involved in meetings to which he felt he should have been invited. He offered me no constructive views or ideas, and I could not rely on him for guidance or support. The better managers I have experienced are those who listen to ideas with interest, question or chal- lenge them and have a clear view of the task in hand. Those managers have enabled me to explore my ideas further and to think things through more thoroughly.

I expect my manager to support and guide me, and to allow me the space to work on my own initiative. At the same time managers have to be accessible and approachable if I need assistance. With many others, I respect those who are confident in their role as managers and who do not hide behind the power that goes with the job. It does help if they show some warmth and concern for the person as well as for the task. That said, some of the better managers can be very cold. I had one manager whom I was able to work with very well in terms of getting the work done. He was clear about the work, offered constructive sugges- tions, and was supportive of my ideas. However, he never once asked me how I was.

Managing and being managed

Are most of the managers doing a bad job, or are the workers' expectations too high? Are managers' ideals about managing conflicting with all those external forces we discussed earlier? Is a manager's perception of what he or she is doing a worker's reality?

> I think part of being a good manager is learning how to deal with the anxiety provoked by having to oversee work done in a way that you wouldn't do it ... a bad manager is someone who cannot delegate but who rather likes ordering people around. It takes some self-confidence and self-knowledge to be a good manager and you also have to have confidence in your workers.

Most people agreed that a manager's job is not an easy one and that managers too need the support of staff, particularly in times of crisis. It was felt that workers should appreciate the heavy workloads of some managers and be prepared to help. However, frustrations were voiced very clearly: some felt it was up to the person being managed to ensure that managers fulfil their tasks and did not see why things like supervision and training should be slotted around their managers' crises or other duties.

Workers generally felt that the manager's personality featured to a large extent in their role and that it was difficult to separate the two. They felt that tasks such as supervision would be ineffective if the manager was distant. This is what one worker had to say:

> The personality of the manager is important in that one has to have a relationship with this person, trust their judgment where necessary and be confident that they know what they are talking about ... if the manager is a naturally manipulative person, the managed person may not feel able to trust or be confident that the manager will support them.

People were asked whether race, gender and sexuality featured in their management relationships. Some felt that it did not, or that it did not need to. Clearly those issues do feature. Managers need to be aware of them.

For one male white manager the issues were real. As a white male he had to make sure that the power he has as a manager does not reinforce institutional racism and sexism. He claims he does this by checking out his motives and by not assuming that the way he sees things is necessarily the right one.

For me as a black woman, surviving as a manager can be hard. I need to deal with both racism and sexism. People either expect you to be a superwoman or a flop. If you are confident, you do not need to be either. Within a manager's relationship with staff, dynamics are governed by many factors, including race, gender, sexuality, etc. Clearly a female worker will respond differently to a female manager, and a black manager may be better able to identify with a black member of staff. A gay manager is in a better position to appreciate the issues of a gay worker. The 'cultural' familiarity may be the contributing factor. One female worker said: 'I like having a woman as a manager because I feel more comfortable ... I think that your manager's attitudes to race, gender, sexuality are very important. When I was "managed" by a man who I knew was sexist, I found the situation undesirable and uncomfortable.' Another worker had this to say: 'as a black woman I feel able to relate to my manager and this is partly due to his sexuality and his understanding of oppressed and minority groups'.

In tackling the issues of sexuality, one gay manager felt that although he thought he was in a good position to challenge heterosexism, he was concerned that because other people are aware of his managerial power they often hide their own personal prejudices. In my experience some would rather transfer to another section than deal with questions such as this.

Conclusion

The managers I have spoken to have defined managing in their own terms and identified the tasks involved. Their definitions do not differ significantly from those described by workers. Expectations marry up to some degree with what managers say they are doing or would like to do, yet many of the experiences of workers are negative ones. Does the reality of managing conflict with our ideals? Perhaps as managers we need to admit that we are not always able to manage in the way we would like to. We get caught up in the crossfire of following directives from 'up above', whilst at the same time supporting staff and looking out for their interests.

Undoubtedly, managers in social work are always called upon to deal with crises or issues that the 'powers that be' decide are more important at the time. Some management tasks do get neglected. Good communication is crucial at this point. Managers need to communicate difficulties to their staff and, where necessary, delegate. As managers we need to take account of our strengths and weaknesses. Feedback from workers should be welcomed. The managers I spoke to thought that they had got it right. The workers felt some had not. Managers are influenced in the way in which they behave as leaders not only by the maturity of their staff in terms of confidence and competence, but also by the job situation and the constraints imposed on them by their organization. They still have to achieve targets, organize workers, motivate, develop and control staff. Managers are sometimes pressured to behave in a task-orientated and directive style in order to meet those demands. It is not easy to get the balance right.

Many thanks to everyone who contributed to this chapter, with a special thanks to the social work team at St Johns Neighbourhood Office.

Questions for consideration

1 One of the tasks for managers in social work is to enable workers to manage others. What are some of the key management tasks involved in that process?

2 How can managers reconcile demands for short-term results and the meeting of clients' needs (which can often mean adopting a directive, autocratic approach) with the expectation that managers care for, and support, staff?

3 From your experience of being managed, what has made the most impact on you as a worker (both negatively and positively)? What would you have done differently?

4 How should concerns for equal opportunity come to feature in management relationships?

5 Is it possible to separate the role from the personality of the manager?

Reference

Blanchard, K. (1988) *Leadership and the One Minute Manager*. London: Fontana.

11

The Daily Round

CELIA PARNELL

Time always seems to be of the essence for the busy social worker. Fitting everything into the working day seems for many to be an impossibility. Expensive time-management courses and planning charts rarely make a difference. The pressure of accumulating work quickly overwhelms good intentions. Some learn how to avoid work and happily leave colleagues to carry an unfair load. Others seem to be able to manage their time and, without a callous disregard for either their colleagues or clients, they match the time available to the demands placed upon them. A third group seem to be buffeted by crisis upon crisis, unable ever to gain a firm grip upon their workload. Few, it seems, are able to choose which of these categories they may come to resemble.

Celia Parnell asks what is it about social work that makes for such difficulties in organizing the daily round. Without simply producing a list of handy hints, the chapter begins by trying to see how a careful analysis of the work can enable a practitioner to begin to manage their time effectively, and how to better understand and deal with the inherent conflict between the need to be flexible in the face of unpredictable demands and yet organized to deal with the routine. Celia returns again and again to the point that there is no magic technique, no time or workload management system which, once adopted, will give the worker endless peace of mind. She describes the feat of organizing time within social work as an art rather than a science.

Like other authors in this book, her strategies involve clarity regarding roles and honesty with clients about boundaries. Her chapter reveals the need for high levels of self-awareness. The amount of time spent on various tasks within social work will, she argues, be as much a product of individual worker styles as the intrinsic needs or demands of the work. Honesty with ourselves about why we always allow our interviews to overrun the allotted time, or why we never get our recording done, or why we rarely get to the team meeting on time, appears to be essential for planning our work.

This chapter is important in focusing our attention on the relationship between the various processes highlighted in earlier chapters. Other authors have had the comparative luxury of placing a single process at the centre of their attention. Celia shows that each task relies on others being achieved, but in the daily round they appear to be in competition with each other for precious time. Perhaps in the end a committed worker can only hope to identify survival strategies. What is certain is that the ever-changing political and social context in which the work takes place makes it impossible to establish a fixed routine or mode of operation which, with minimal alteration, might suffice for a lifetime in social work. That said, it need not be a reason for failing to address this central issue in our professional lives. This chapter shows that managing our time is not something that comes after professional judgments have been made; rather, they go hand in hand with each other.

* * *

On being asked to write this chapter, I initially set out to describe a 'typical' social work day. I soon realized that this would be misleading, as there is so little that is routine or predictable in social work, and so much that would have been missed out. Instead, I have approached the subject by describing the various activities in which social workers are engaged, the specific difficulties that they have to contend with in organizing the working day, and how social workers tackle this in practice.

As my own recent experience has been with local authorities, working with children and families, I will base many of my comments on work in that setting. I believe that my experience has relevance to workers in other agencies and with different client groups as, whilst some of the tasks will be different, many of the dilemmas are shared.

In most social work agencies, workers are employed for a 35–40 hours week, usually within office hours: that is, approximately nine to five with an hour for lunch. Most agencies do not pay overtime, and there is an expectation that any extra hours worked will be taken off as time in lieu. The rules about how this process is agreed and organized vary: some teams have a formal system of recording extra hours worked and lieu time taken; others have no system other than a general understanding that workers will be accountable for their own time management; others do not acknowledge that it is necessary to work outside normal office hours and therefore there is no official permission to take lieu time.

Statutory social work agencies have emergency duty teams which deal with crises and new referrals which arise outside office hours. However, few social workers find it possible to confine all of their work to prescribed hours: some clients are only available after 5 p.m., and some pieces of work which are started during the day will need to be carried over into the evening. Anyone in social work must accept that it is a job that can involve some anti-social hours and that these are sometimes, but not always, unpredictable.

Balanced against the requirement to provide a flexible service which adapts to the needs of individual cases is the necessity of office cover during agreed hours, so that a predictable service is available to the public and for other agencies to make referrals and discuss cases. Most agencies organize some form of system whereby a duty worker is available during office hours to take messages and deal with new referrals, but it is also necessary for clients and other agencies to have some idea of times when they can contact individual workers about their cases.

As I shall go on to describe, there are aspects of social work which make it a difficult activity to quantify. One case may take up eight hours per week, but another only one hour per month of a worker's time. It all depends on the nature of the case, the method of work undertaken and a worker's own style and pace. Attempts have been made to devise 'workload management' systems. These attempt to measure the volume of work and share it equally amongst team members, but are generally agreed to be only rough measures which most practitioners acknowledge have only limited usefulness in keeping work within manageable limits. There is no agreement about optimal workloads for social workers. Some agencies which do not have statutory duties are in the position of agreeing a limit to the number of pieces of work which they will undertake at any one time. Social services departments have a variety of statutory responsibilities which oblige them to make a response to the majority of referrals. With the implementation of the Children Act 1989, the scope of these duties has considerably increased and, in cases of child protection, there is a requirement to make assessments and to act within a shorter timescale. For example, when statutory intervention was necessary to protect a child under previous legislation, a Place of Safety Order could have been obtained for up to 28 days; under the Children Act an Emergency Protection Order can only be granted for up to 8 days. During this time the social worker must make an assessment of the risks involved in returning the child home and, if necessary, prepare a case for application to the court for an Interim Care Order.

Social work literature offers little practical guidance to students on strategies for organizing their time, and student placements with their limited workloads rarely prepare new workers adequately for this aspect of the job. Theories about time management generally fail to take account of the unique factors in social work which complicate the process. Social work managers, often over-worked and stressed, seldom offer more than sympathy; workers who run into difficulties are readily blamed for poor time management. Responsibility for organizing their working day is largely a matter for the workers' own initiative, and a wide range of approaches can be observed, from those workers whose diaries are fully booked to those who make as few plans as possible and wait for events and the demands of others to structure their time.

Both of these approaches have their difficulties. A fully planned diary leaves no room for handling the unanticipated which is a feature of most settings; lack of planning leads to chaotic working and uncompleted tasks. Workers who do not take responsibility for planning their time at all end up feeling out of control, whilst clients and colleagues feel let down, dissatisfied and angry.

As with most professionals, a social worker's day consists of a balance of fixed commitments which are prearranged and a certain flexibility to plan their own time in respect of work allocated to them. Some commitments, such as attendance at court to give evidence, are seen by the agency or team as compulsory, whilst others (for example, an agreement to give a talk to a group of volunteers) are seen as discretionary. New workers need to be clear about which is which, and also to understand their team and agency culture: what is the attitude to missing the team meeting; what are the expectations about 'extras' like student supervision; will there be willingness to cover for you if you have made an appointment that coincides with your office duty?

It would be reasonable for social work students to expect that the majority of their time would be taken up by direct work with clients: this is what the job is all about. However, an analysis of a social worker's diary will show that this will vary from week to week, probably accounting for no more than a quarter of the working week. Workload management systems which attempt to quantify the proportion of time spent on client contact are relatively unpopular as social workers do not like to accept the reality of this, for many subjectively feel that they have spent much more time with clients than is actually the case.

Other activities which take up social workers' time can be broadly categorized as liaison; meetings; recording; report writing and administration; and training and development. I will go on to describe the kind of things that social workers have to think about in dividing their time between these activities.

Client contact

No two social work referrals are the same. They may present similarly (e.g., a request for a day care resource), but the process which follows will have variables according to the personal characteristics of the client and his or her situation. The personal style of the worker will equally determine how the case is handled, even within fairly prescriptive procedures. One of my hardest lessons on becoming a first line manager was that a case allocated within my team could have five different outcomes, depending on which worker was responsible for it. I knew that one worker would stick rigidly to the narrow remit of the referral, assess whether the client met the criteria for the resource, complete the necessary administration and close the case. Another would be more likely to encourage the client to embark on his or her life history, to uncover all sorts of additional problems, and to extend the original referral to a piece of intensive counselling. I do not intend to make a judgment about the merits of either style, only to point out that there are individual differences which have different time implications.

Whatever the nature of the case and the style of work, it is essential for workers to have a broad plan for contact in each case. This may seem too obvious to be stated but, because of other pressures on time, it is all too easy to put off visits which you know should be made but which you have not actually planned, to allow contact to drift, or to spend a disproportionate amount of time with the most demanding (or the most rewarding) clients to the detriment of those with an equal need.

In adherence to a general philosophy of respect for others, and specifically in keeping with the principle of the Children Act of partnership with parents, most social workers would probably agree that clients are entitled to be included in discussion about, or at the very least to be made aware of, the way we plan to respond to their request for a service or to carry out our statutory duties in respect of their family. It is generally discourteous to arrive unannounced at people's homes and then to expect them to be prepared to discuss highly personal matters in an interview for which we, but not they, are prepared. There are, of course, occasions when unannounced visits are necessary – for example, to establish the facts at the outset of a child protection enquiry or to monitor standards of care – but the intention and purpose of this method of visiting should be shared with the family. When in these circumstances no appointments are made, the intended frequency of visiting should be explicit to the worker to avoid drift. My experience is that it is better to record in your diary the intention to visit, even if this is not shared with the client. Cases where unplanned visits get endlessly deferred can be a source of much anxiety to social workers, and the client is not getting a service.

In thinking about how time is spent on client contact, it is important to take into account the length as well as the frequency of visits, and to attempt to put some boundaries on this aspect of the use of your time, for reasons which can be helpful to both worker and client. Some workers will make six visits during the course of a morning, whilst others will make only one in the same space of time. Again, it is a matter of courtesy to give some indication to the client of how long you will be able to spend with them; it is also a survival skill for social workers which requires a certain amount of self-confidence, sensitivity and assertiveness to put into practice. Some clients will spend an hour's session carefully avoiding the main issue, and only when you say that you must leave do they produce some sensitive information in an attempt to keep your attention for longer. This can be hard to resist for an inexperienced worker or one whose professional ego is boosted by a sense of having 'enabled' the client to share something so important to them. However, it is a poor learning experience for clients to find that their most personal information can be traded for attention, and it is unlikely to be dealt with helpfully. As you begin to look furtively at your watch and realize that you are late for the next appointment, it becomes increasingly difficult to find the right point to end the interview. It is probably better both for the quality of service and the worker's peace of mind to end the session at the agreed time, to acknowledge the importance of what they are telling you and to confirm that you will think about it carefully and will pick it up with them at the next session. If you have agreed the length of the session with them at the outset, this is less likely to be experienced as rejecting.

This is not so easy to achieve in practice as it sounds in theory. Deprived and desperate people will have unconscious strategies for trying to delay your departure, including tears, more information, not 'hearing' your ending of the interview and even, on occasions, threats of self-harm, harm towards children or disclosures of abuse. It is a matter of skilled judgment to decide when it is safe to leave as planned and when you need to stay or to take some other action. In my experience, it is a mistake to make solo visits to the most vulnerable clients after office hours, unless there is at least an agreed back-up of a phone call to the senior officer to report on the outcome of the visit. I recall visiting a woman who insisted that she would not let me leave her house until I had told her the whereabouts of her daughter whom I had recently removed from her care. Had I not been able to contact my team leader I might still have been there. Fortunately I was able to persuade her that I was unable to take this decision alone, and she eventually agreed that I could contact the team leader, who arrived with assistance to ensure that I was able to leave the house.

Having suggested that it is important to have a plan of client contact, I would emphasize that it is equally important to accept that the nature of the job is such that your planning will sometimes be disrupted. It is probable that you will be working with some people who crave attention and make frequent demands on your time, whose lives are crisis-ridden and who have difficulty in working to a plan. Understanding the source of someone's neediness does not necessarily make them easier to deal with. The frustration of working with someone who contacts you several times in a day, and who seems unable to act on your advice or derive comfort from your sympathy can be extremely high, no matter how much insight you have into the reasons for their behaviour. But it can perhaps at least help you to manage your irritation and to make a more appropriate response aimed at helping them to express their needs in a way that is less likely to bring a rejecting response.

Equally disruptive in the planning of your day are those reluctant clients who avoid contact with you. When you are under pressure, their avoidance can be very convenient. It would be easy to fail to follow up the appointment either in person or by letter, and to close the case labelling them as 'unco-operative', even when it could have been anticipated that they would be hard to engage. In the same way, when you are particularly busy, it is tempting to knock quietly on a door and return quickly to the office to note 'no reply' on the file.

Social work in most settings is characterized by crises. In work with children and families these arise most commonly in respect of child protection work and juvenile justice. Often when you are out of the office for even a short space of time, messages can pile up at an alarming rate, each saying that they require an urgent response. These vary from an unspecified request to call a health visitor to a demand to visit a family because their electricity has been disconnected; or notification that a child you are working with is in hospital following a suicide attempt to information that one of the adolescents on your caseload is at the police station; and a note from your team leader reminding you that your report to the adoption panel must be handed in today. Somehow you have to prioritize your responses to these messages, and fit them in around your planned work.

Allegations of child abuse must be dealt with promptly, as must any referral which suggests that someone is at risk. Most departments' procedures indicate a timescale for responding, and an expectation that the case will be investigated by two experienced workers together, one of whom may be a police officer in certain circumstances. Such investigations can be both time-consuming and emotionally harrowing.

Juvenile justice is particularly unpredictable in its demands. The requirements of the Police and Criminal Evidence Act can demand that a social worker attends the police station to witness the interviewing of a juvenile if parents are unable or unwilling to; or you may need to pick up a young person who has absconded from care, sometimes from the other end of the country, only for them to jump out of the car at the traffic lights once you have returned them to their home town! You need a particularly sanguine and optimistic personality to maintain a positive approach to your work if you have many cases like that.

Individual workers and teams have a variety of approaches for dealing with a crisis. If a highly individualized approach is taken, it is likely that the crisis will have to wait for the client's own worker to deal with it; if there is a team approach, it may be dealt with on the basis of availability or familiarity with the case. This relies on good communication between colleagues, trust in one another's judgment, willingness to share, and an adequate system of record keeping so that colleagues can make an informed response.

Social work is an infuriatingly self-generating occupation. The more work you undertake with and on behalf of families, the more people will expect of you. Those workers whose clients perceive them as unhelpful or disinterested are less likely to be approached for advice and support. If people identify you as helpful, sympathetic and reliable, they are likely to seek your opinion on a problem or your support in a crisis.

Liaison

The above principle applies equally to those aspects of the job that are concerned with working together with other professionals. Workers who actively seek to make links with other agencies in order to share information and opinions with them are likely to be consulted more often. It is therefore quite possible to limit the amount of liaison that you have to deal with by presenting yourself as unhelpful or unreliable, which is not a time management strategy that I would recommend!

In child care, liaison with other agencies is not only a question of good practice, but is required by government guidelines and local procedures. For example, this involves making and maintaining links with others who are working with children: health visitors, school nurses, GPs, teachers, psychologists, child and family psychiatrists and the police. It also involves advocating on behalf of families with other agencies, such as the DSS, Housing or Education. The demands that this type of work can make on social workers' time can be considerable and difficult to manage. Many of the other professionals with whom you need to keep in touch are also working with people in the community and, like social workers, their office is a base to which they return from time to time, not a place where they can be reliably contacted. At those times, when you and they are most likely to be in the office (i.e., first thing in the morning or around lunchtime), telephone lines are invariably engaged as everyone tries to ring one another. Social workers often defensively note in their written records their unsuccessful attempts to contact colleagues by phone. It has always seemed to me to be worth following up an unsuccessful telephone call with a letter asking the person to contact you and saying when you will be available.

Establishing good working links can be time-consuming initially, but can ultimately save you time as assessments are shared and duplication avoided. They can also be an invaluable source of support, reducing the need for you to spend time seeking this through other channels. A health visitor who has shared your experience of trying to work with a particularly idiosyncratic family is likely to be a better source of comfort over a cup of tea when you need to offload your frustrations and may be more willing to listen to your endless anecdotes than bored colleagues who respond with 'Not the M-s again!'

Meetings

Attendance at meetings is a regular feature of most social workers' weeks. This is an aspect of social work which is less reliant on individual initiative, as many meetings are prearranged with an expectation of attendance. Meetings which social workers in child-care teams, for example, often have to attend include case reviews, planning meetings and child protection case conferences. They may also have to present cases to adoption and placement panels, say, which fullfil a gatekeeping function to specific resources. There is little flexibility around these arrangements other than the possibility that a senior officer or colleague might take your place in an emergency.

Most social work teams have a weekly meeting for information sharing and the discussion of issues of common concern. This can also incorporate allocation, where decisions are made about the distribution of new work within the team. Some workers will view the team meeting as optional, and may try to use the time to catch up on other work. Whether or not this is endorsed will depend upon the attitude of colleagues and the team leader. In my experience, lack of commitment to team meetings can lead to resentment between workers, unfair distribution of work (not always to the advantage of the absent worker!), poor communication and difficulties in achieving shared tasks such as covering the duty rota, taking messages for one another and co-working.

Attendance at Juvenile Court could be described within the context of meetings, having the same features of being a fixed appointment involving other people. This is an extremely time-consuming commitment over which social workers have no control. You often spend several hours waiting outside the court, only to find the case is adjourned. There is little that you can do to make constructive use of this time, and the only positive approach I can find is to view it as (a) time to spend with your client, and (b) time to socialize with other workers in the same situation. No amount of positive thinking can effectively reduce the irritation at wasting so much time when you have other work waiting.

Training, development and support

Time set aside for training presents a particular double bind for social workers, and managers' attitudes to it can be ambiguous. On the one hand, most workers recognize their need for training, but when it is provided they often feel that it is not a high priority, or perhaps because it is enjoyable and for their own benefit they regard it as self-indulgent. Trainers often complain that workers cancel their place on a course at the last minute because they have prioritized something else, or that they intend to miss parts of the course to carry out urgent work. I think that time booked for training should be viewed in the same way as that set aside for annual leave; you are not available for work, and therefore the team will have to manage without you. However, this requires a similar attitude from managers, and it should not be left to individual workers' ability to assert their rights to take up training opportunities.

Most social work agencies expect that regular supervision should be structured into workers' time at an agreed frequency. This tends to be another appointment which is all too often regarded as movable or optional, and is given a low priority in competition with other demands. It is worth checking out the team leader's attitude to supervision and the team's experience before you accept a job. Other developmental opportunities, like student supervision or developing training skills, are often also given low priority. It may require real assertiveness or self-discipline to make space for them.

Most social workers are members of teams. This is partly for administrative reasons, but is also an acknowledgment of the need to create an environment where workers can get support from one another, both formally and informally. It is somewhere they can share ideas, learn from one another and contribute to mutual development. This requires time to be made for activities that will facilitate team-building. Some aspects of team support – such as team meetings, case discussions and team training – will be planned and diaried. However, much support and learning will take place in an *ad hoc* way within the team room, such as providing immediate support to a colleague returning from a harrowing visit, pooling ideas on a difficult case or sharing an amusing anecdote. This immediate support can be invaluable to workers under stress; it can equally become a source of stress for others if some workers' need for support is so great that they continually erode time that colleagues have set aside for other work. You need to be aware of how much you are able to give in this respect, and to put some boundaries down if necessary.

Administration

A large proportion of social workers' time is (or is expected to be) given to administrative tasks, recording and report writing. There is a temptation to see these as of secondary importance rather than as an integral part of the work. Few social workers seem to be good organizers in this respect, and it is a constant headache to team leaders to ensure that manual and computer records are kept up to date, and that deadlines for reports are met. Time allocated for paperwork is often eroded by other tasks.

Child-care work is characterized by a considerable amount of paperwork. Where there is no deadline with, for example, case recording, a piece of work is inevitably given low priority and this leads to the common situation of records being months out of date. Few workers are unconcerned about this, and it becomes an additional source of stress. Many resort to writing up their records at home.

In addition to those issues for time management which are specific to social work, workers have to contend with all of the general interruptions which can seem to conspire to disrupt their day: the car breaking down, a sick child at home, the office fire drill, or the duty officer ringing in sick.

The organization of social work offices seldom seems designed to assist with efficient time management. Shortages of telephone lines cause delay in making phone calls; inadequate parking space leads to late arrivals at the office, or meetings disrupted as participants appear after the agreed time. There is little that social workers can do to overcome these obstacles other than to point out to management the effects on their efficiency.

Social work training offers little to assist workers with the organization of their time, and supervisors often feel helpless to offer concrete suggestions. In my experience, there are a number of practical and attitudinal approaches which can help workers to feel less overwhelmed and more in control of their working day.

Survival strategies

The basis of a strategy for survival is the acceptance that social work contains unique elements which will make it difficult always to stick to your plans. This implies the development of skills to deal confidently with those occasions when plans have to be changed without developing a sense of unreliability. It is essential at the outset, when negotiating with a client how and when you will carry out your work with them, to explain that occasionally you may need to cancel appointments. It is nearly always possible to at least get a colleague to call round with a message or to ask the receptionist to apologize on your behalf. In doing this, it is important to recognize that some people are so damaged and fragile that they will read a message of rejection into any change of plan and will see it as confirmation of their own insignificance. Unless you are able to recognize this, and deal with it openly, the client may be too upset or angry to continue to work with you. However, if you are able to anticipate their response, you can deal with it proactively and sensitively, rather than simply generating in yourself a feeling of guilt about missed appointments which can be disabling in future work. One social worker was pleased to be told by a client that she was different from previous workers who had visited her. She waited with anticipation to be told how she was more sensitive, sympathetic, understanding, etc., and was very deflated to be told 'At least you come on time'. On reflection, this was the quality that the client had found most valuable, and it should not be under-rated.

There are times when it would be easiest to respond to the most demanding clients, thereby neglecting those who have an equal need. It is important to have sufficient professional skills and confidence to make a reasoned judgment as to which actions are urgent and which can wait, otherwise you become exhausted, demoralized and ineffective.

Social workers need to accept that they have responsibility for prioritizing the use of their time. This is something that can and should be shared with the team leader initially as it is part of the process of developing your professional role. In most agencies, level three social workers are expected to have an understanding of how the agency prioritizes different activities and to make independent decisions about the organization of their day. It is necessary to understand the agency's priorities and statutory requirements, including rules about how up-to-date recording should be; the minimum visiting frequency to children in family placements; expectations of the frequency of visits to children on the child protection register; which deadlines are fixed, and which may be negotiable. Some of these are laid down by law or agency procedure, while others will be learnt through experience and discussion. Throughout this chapter, I have emphasized the importance of planning. The elusive balance between planning and flexibility is as much concerned with the art of the use of yourself in your professional role as with the science of time management. Whilst there are practical, tangible elements of good organization that will help you to keep sane and on top of your work most of the time, the translation of these into the practice of social work relies on a strong sense of self-awareness that will inform you about your own responses to demands made on you when you are working under stress.

Finally, looking after yourself and ensuring that your own needs are met are essential elements in getting through the day. There is an infinite amount of work to be done, and you are the only person who can effectively put boundaries around the amount of time you are prepared to spend at work. As I suggested at the outset, it is unrealistic to assume that your job will be carried out between the hours of nine and five. It is not a job that you are likely to survive and feel creative in unless you can clearly define your leisure time and ensure that you make opportunities to relax and forget about your work for a while.

Questions for consideration

1   What are your own usual coping strategies when there are a lot of demands on your time? How can you use this piece of self-awareness to ensure that you develop a professional approach to time management?

2   What are the particular features of social work that militate against the keeping of a well-ordered diary?

3   What criteria would you use in prioritizing different activities?

4   What can (a) you, and (b) your agency, do if you feel that the volume of work is unmanageable?

5   Set out a statement, which you could use as a basis for negotiation with your line manager, outlining your expectations of how they and the agency can assist you in managing your time.

12

Making Sense of Social Working

PAM CARTER, TONY JEFFS AND MARK K. SMITH

None of the contributors to this book portrays social work as an easy option. Each, without overplaying their hand, indicates the extent to which social workers experience pressure and must construct survival strategies. The need to survive, to get through the day, is a sub-text that cannot be brushed aside for it continuously shapes practice and determines priorities. Although the solutions are sometimes collective, such as finding time to talk to colleagues or seeking ways of working collaboratively rather than in isolation, many survival strategies are often highly personal. This should not divert our attention, however, from the structural causes that create the tensions and stress within the work. The political and social factors that shape the working environment in which social workers operate cannot be overlooked, even in a text that commences from the analysis of individual practice.

All the contributors, although focusing upon their own practice, nevertheless highlight the difficulty of working with clients who have pressing needs, such as individuals and groups for whom resources always seem stretched, and who invariably have insufficient money; who are often burdened by ill-health; who are frequently poorly housed, even homeless; and in far too many instances, rightly or wrongly, who see themselves as victims of uncaring bureaucracies. Undoubtedly the plight of many of those whom social workers encounter as clients has deteriorated in recent years. Stigmatization of the poor has become commonly used as a deliberate policy: to drive people into low paid jobs; to discourage the claiming of benefits; or to disguise the structural causes of poverty and encourage the acceptance of individual explanations (Oppenheim, 1990; Cohen *et al.*, 1992; Craig, 1992). Many social workers are less and less able to offer material help. Agency funding that is accessible to a social worker to help alleviate immediate problems has tended to diminish. Similarly, opportunities to overcome client problems via practical advice as to where, for example, employment can be secured, resources obtained or help found, have become rarer. The introduction of the Social Fund has for many turned financial assistance into a cruel lottery (DSS, 1992); cuts in local housing budgets and the wholesale disposal of stock in certain areas make it virtually impossible for some clients to find accommodation; reductions in grant aid and local authority funding mean that there are fewer and fewer full-time specialist workers capable of helping with welfare rights, legal problems or advice; each of these individually and collectively makes for a discouraging and debilitating climate in which to work.

Within social work itself similar changes have taken place. Through talking to workers with long memories it is possible to gauge the extent of this. The physical standards of the workplace have in some cases deteriorated: in many areas offices have become more cramped and shabby; the menus and decor of some residential homes now seem less inviting; and petty restrictions designed to save pennies seem to have multiplied everywhere. In addition projects and initiatives that once offered valued services – such as a holiday playscheme down the road, a respite care programme for the town, or a community resource centre for the neighbourhood – have been starved of funds, run down and all too often either closed by diktat or allowed to collapse. Some readers may question this gloomy picture of deteriorating conditions and standards. It has to be recognized that it is possible to point to improvements that have taken place in recent years. Better working environments and more attractive day and residential settings are to be found. Overall, however, material improvements have been secured at the expense of staffing levels and reductions in the volume and range of provision. In some instances the statutory has survived through the decimation of voluntary and community initiatives; in other localities the voluntary appears to have flourished when observed from the perspective of workers in the statutory sector. There is no universal rule of thumb in these matters, except that for all there is a realization that, even if their experience has not worsened, they are aware that it has for others.

Inevitably social workers are drawn into the process of managing and controlling resources. Who has to tell the family that after next month there will be no respite care, or that the home-care will cost more and visit less often? Usually in these (and a multitude of other daily) encounters it is the front-line social worker. They endure the embarrassment; they are on the receiving end of client anger and frustration. All this is occurring whilst fundamental changes are taking place in their own employment conditions. The long-term decline in the value of the student grant continues, whilst secondment and sponsorship become ever more difficult to secure. The result is that more and more social workers are forced to pay for, or subsidize, their own initial and further training. Meanwhile those entering the profession, and many already within it, find that their conditions of employment are deteriorating. Short-term contracts are increasingly being offered; part-time posts replace full-time ones; and few are the social workers who have not by now seen colleagues re-deployed against their will, threatened with, or actually being made redundant. As local authorities become 'enablers' rather than suppliers of services, so more and more social workers find themselves propelled into employment in privatized agencies and voluntary organizations, some of the latter operating on the basis of similar criteria to the former. Social work jobs are disappearing to be replaced by community care managers. The ways in which this is changing individual and collective perceptions of the role and purpose of social work is something that has so far received scant attention. How social workers will adjust their attitudes and value systems to working within the 'for profit sector' is a question that as yet cannot be answered. Historically, training has assumed that the overwhelming majority of workers will be employed by statutory agencies and a minority by familiar voluntary and charitable bodies. This pattern will apply less and less in the future. What was once seen as a secure job with prospects is becoming by the day less so. Is it any wonder that, when all these changes are put together, tempers may more readily become frayed or that research indicates increased levels of stress amongst social workers (King, 1991)?

Organizational change

The loss of resources has to be set beside growing demand, much of which emanates from increased unemployment and under-employment as well demographic changes (Schorr, 1992). The combination of all these has tended to make the lot of social workers more onerous; but these are only partial explanations for the rising levels of stress and dissatisfaction so often conveyed in conversations with social workers. Other factors have to be taken into account, not least the constant climate of uncertainty linked to organizational and administrative change described by Chapman in Chapter 2. It often seems impossible to achieve stability within the personal social services. Departments, teams and offices always appear to be undergoing or on the brink of a major review and re-structuring. Why this is the case varies according to different circumstances: sometimes it is management trying to justify their existence, or to create a means of isolating an awkward or incompetent member of staff.

Re-organization can also be the end product of legislation and policy changes: examples of this must include the re-organization that followed the Seebohm Report (1968). This led, along with the restructuring of local authorities, to the unification of a number of disparate departments and agencies, creating in the process new, large, generic statutory social work departments (Hall, 1976). The story of the post-Seebohm years may be conceived of as intially a series of attempts to implement the reforms, followed by a seeking of ways to modify them and finally to undermine and unravel the Seebohm structure. In recent years efforts to fragment the departments and bring the workers closer to community and clients have frequently been reversed. Increasingly common have been moves to return to specialization, accompanied by a concentration on statutory provision and services targeted on those perceived as being in most 'urgent and extreme need'. Social work's ambition to offer a broad preventive and generic service to all those in need has to a large extent been jettisoned in this process. A significant strand in this relates to child protection. A number of important cases concerning child abuse and malpractice within the residential sector have led to the issuing of government guidelines and circulars. These have required or stimulated re-organization in order to prevent their re-occurrence. Finally many changes have arisen from overtly political motivation, in particular an ideological determination to create a free market in welfare, to restructure family life and to reinforce individual responsibility. Within probation, as Marshall (Chapter 5) points out, this has meant that workers have been forced to re-orientate their approach, moving from a welfare model to one that lays greater emphasis upon control and punishment, and thus forcing clients to confront their 'criminal behaviour' (Home Office, 1988; Allan, 1990; Holdaway and Mantle, 1992). Externally imposed policy changes can lead to a re-orientation of the work. Often these can erode the autonomy of the worker. In one instance sustained interrogation of practice allowed the worker to continue to operate according to a value system that she found compatable with her earlier modes of practice.

The implementation of the reforms advocated by the Griffiths Report (1988) on care in the community has had a dramatic impact upon the structure of departments and the role of social workers, encouraging the move from direct delivery of services by departments to the purchasing and monitoring of non-statutory provision and altering the employment conditions of many workers, requiring social workers to become more overtly managers of resources and cash-limited budgets. These changes are not, and cannot be, final. They will not produce the longed-for stability. Local government re-organization, the impact of European legislation, the free movement of labour and welfare harmonization will all continue to change both the context and experience of social work practice. Technological change will also constantly restructure the working day, the composition of the labour force and decision-making processes. At a macro-level, changes within the international economic system along with the interplay of political forces will produce unheralded shifts in terms of the types of need and demand which will confront social workers. Simultaneously, new and reinvigorated oppositional forces will confront and challenge existing practice and structures. Making sense of such changes requires that social workers acquire an active sense of their own history. Marshall (Chapter 5) provides an example of how current practice can only be effectively interrogated when it is historically contextualized. A sense of history is a vital aid, and not simply in relation to the analysis and interpretation of macro policy. Chapman (Chapter 2), in building the 'team', had to take account of the structures that had gone before to acknowledge, recognize and work with the 'climate of leftover feelings' that the new colleagues brought with them. Work with clients demands a similar respect for, and awareness of, their histories.

Undermining the social worker

Organizational uncertainty undermines the self-confidence of social workers. However, many also feel threatened by other factors which we have yet to consider. Often, it seems, only estate agents and double-glazing salespersons have a lower public standing than social workers. Why is this? Partly, low status is a reflection of the public image of the 'kinds of people' who use their services. Respectable middle-class and responsible citizens may employ a therapist, but would never at a dinner party let slip that they were a social work case. It is a view that clients themselves are not immune to. As Rees found in one not atypical interview, 'A person that has worked hard all his life is not aware of these things. I thought social work was for the down-and-outs' (1978, p. 124). Such reluctance has been compounded by the emergence of substantive evidence that sexual abuse occurs within the nicest of families (Campbell, 1988; MacLeod and Saraga, 1988). This has required social workers stepping outside their traditional remit of monitoring the poor and 'inadequate'. Child abuse demands that they now police all families, and for perhaps the first time they may force their way into the homes of the 'respectable' middle and upper working class.

All social workers have suffered as a result of the attacks by politicians and commentators on the welfare system. The portrayal of them as encouraging dependency and a lack of self-reliance amongst the 'new underclass' (Murray, 1984; Mann, 1992) whilst being profligate with scarce public funds has encouraged defensiveness and the emergence of a siege mentality. Unlike prison, police and probation officers, social workers are a group *par excellence* who neither produce wealth nor protect society from the 'forces of evil'. Worse, we are told by sections of the media that here is a group who lend succour and support to the 'enemy within' (Franklin, 1989; Franklin and Parton, 1991).

Unfortunately not all criticism of social workers is without justification. The dangerous, incompetent and abusing social worker is not simply a myth conjured forth by an unsympathetic media. Court cases and enquiries have continually provided isolated but persistent reminders that social work contains its share of 'bad apples', and that considerable collusion amongst colleagues and management has allowed seriously damaging behaviour to continue unchecked for substantial periods of time (Levy and Kahan, 1991). The reasons for this are complex. However, such behaviour often seems to be linked to three issues. The first is a commonly encountered, but misplaced, interpretation of professional loyalty: one that sees concern and care for colleagues, their needs and feelings as deserving priority over those of clients. A second is a misreading of the role of trade unions and professional organizations. Here it is deemed essential to protect the jobs and status of members at all costs, irrespective of the degree to which this may operate against the best interests of those vulnerable to exploitation. This is, of course, not merely a problem experienced within social work. In higher education such bodies have consistently protected from dismissal those who sexually exploit students (Carter and Jeffs, 1992). Amongst therapists (Rutter, 1989) and psychologists (Llewelyn, 1992) similar closure is widely encountered. This is in part an almost understandable response to a perception widely canvassed amongst social workers that they have to survive in a predominantly hostile environment, and that a criticism of one is a criticism of all. A tendency for this to occur is not unique. Such closure is a feature of all professions: as Adam Smith noted in the eighteenth century, 'People of the same trade seldom meet together even for merriment and diversion, but the conversation ends in a conspiracy against the public' (quoted in Wilding, 1982, p. 15). Such explanations should not be allowed to be used as a blanket excuse.

Choice and control in practice

Post-Seebohm literature had a tendency to emphasize the extent to which social workers' practice is restricted and constrained, and to recount how they are denied 'autonomous control as practitioners over their work ... are closely supervised by their superiors in their day-to-day work' (Abbott and Wallace, 1990, p. 4). This interpretation is scarcely borne out by the accounts of practice presented within this text. What emerges from these is the extent to which practitioners, rightly or wrongly, perceive themselves as having a significant measure of control over the ways in which they choose to undertake their work. Within Mann's contribution (Chapter 6), what emerges is the extent to which she was responsible for devising appropriate rules and patterns of behaviour, rather than merely operating those imposed by management decree. Within a constantly changing organizational context it neverthe-less remains the case that social work is characterized as an occupation by its ability to control substantive areas of practice. This measure of freedom has always been challenged by employers and politicians, who continuously seek to circumscribe the autonomy of social workers. However, the very nature of the work prevents them from achieving the control they desire. Despite radical changes social workers continue to be employed within 'front-line' organizations where the monitoring, supervision and control of individual staff remains tenuous (D. Smith, 1965; G. Smith, 1979).

At the beginning of this chapter we felt it was important to contextu-alize any consideration of practice by reference to the political and social changes that have an impact on the daily lives of social workers. Combined with these changes, the very nature of social work means that the practice recounted in this text is characterized by uncertainty and unpredictability. As Parnell notes in Chapter 11, it is impossible to describe a typical 'social work day'. Yet paradoxically both uncertainty and unpredictability present social workers with opportunities to exercise creative and responsible judgment or, alternatively, to collude with unethical behaviour and bad practice. Jordan presents an account of practice recounted by a student. This concerned the way in which residential staff would resort to punitive solutions in the face of provocative behaviour, despite the fact that such solutions were frequently in opposition to their expressed values. The student described the way in which these responses were rationalized by the staff as a legitimate use of authority; nevertheless, such situations left a strong residual sense of discomfort: 'ultimately he always had a sense of bad faith about such rationalisations. He was conscious that these were exactly the same things (or more pompous versions of the same things) that parents, teachers, employers, wives, neighbours, magistrates and officials had said previously about these clients' (Jordan, 1984, p. 152).

Public exposure of poor practice has increasingly produced technocratic responses from politicians and senior managers anxious to protect themselves from association with, or blame for, the mistakes of those beneath them in the hierarchy. Procedural manuals, inspection and quality control, and competency-based training schemes all seek to transform social work from an art to a technical exercise. The fatal flaw within all these technocratic approaches is that they obscure a central characteristic of social work practice which, as Pithouse argues, 'is an inherently "invisible" trade that cannot be "seen" without engaging in the workers' own routines for understanding their complex occupational terrain' (1987, p. 2). This means that unless attempts to maintain and improve standards are founded upon an unambiguous understanding of the lived experience of social workers, they will be doomed to failure. External attempts to achieve this end also suffer because they all too often are linked to a simultaneous desire by management to reduce expenditure, staffing levels and worker autonomy. Even where this is not the case, as Kelly notes, 'most inspectors acknowledge it is difficult to stimulate change from outside' (1992, p. 17). An understanding of the lived experience will, as we noted in the first chapter, be unlikely to emerge without the interrogation of their practice by workers themselves. By constantly 'returning to', 'attending to' and 'evaluating' experience it becomes possible to undertake independent analysis of policy and to construct models of practice that equate with the values of the practitioner, and which make for the well-being of the client rather than organizational convenience. An essential part of this is workers scrutinizing their own subjective perceptions and judgments within a myriad of structural relationships. For example, continuous attention to the complex dynamics of race, gender, class, age, (dis)ability and sexuality is a prerequisite for professional practice which aims to promote human flourishing.

From the initial chapter onwards contributors have demonstrated the importance of social workers acquiring, through the analysis of their own practice, a repertoire of useful routines. It is important to distinguish between those routines that are imposed and which remain outside the control of the worker, resistant to adaptation, and others which are incorporated and utilized within the repertoire of the practitioner. We can recognize the ways in which they simultaneously use accumulated routines to clarify their thinking concerning the purpose of their endeavours whilst providing a means by which they can monitor effectiveness. The starting point for this process may be a task that at first glance appears to be somewhat mundane. Record keeping, as Little (Chapter 3) shows, is something that can be perceived as imposed, onerous and bureaucratic, or which can be elevated to the creative and significant as something capable of illuminating client needs as well as the impact, progress and change wrought by intervention. Turner (Chapter 9), in similar vein, shows how supervision, which might easily be reduced to the status of managerial monitoring, can present a valuable opportunity for enhancing the effectiveness of the worker. Both indicate that, far from being luxuries which detract from the 'real work', these activities (like other familiar processes) can contribute directly to improved practice and extend worker autonomy, providing a mechanism for the interrogation of the daily round and the partial resolution of the inevitable ethical dilemmas and conflicts that occur. In so doing social workers are constructing afresh their essential craft, and cultivating those attributes that they require to do their job well.

Ethical dilemmas

The dilemmas and conflicts which hover at the shoulder of all social workers during every encounter with both clients and colleagues can best

be seen as ethical ones. As Shardlow says, 'questions about values ... per-
meate the whole context of social work practice' (1989, pp. 2–3), for
they relate to both relationships and the allocation of scarce resources,
time and financial. Social workers have to make choices; that is fundamentally what they are employed to do. This will include choices, for
example, regarding their mode of intervention which, as Boyd and
Skittrall (Chapter 8) show, will always represent an explicit or implicit
preference. For them the use of informal educational methods is based
not on grounds simply of technical efficiency, but upon a belief that such
a mode of intervention is ethically superior and that it is more likely to
enhance the independence and self-esteem of both the individual partici-
pant and the collective. Much of the harsh and cruel treatment meted out
to young people in care (Carlen and Wardhaugh, 1991), the callousness
towards the elderly (Marshall, 1989), the failure to recognize the specific
needs of black people (Dominelli, 1988; Williams, 1989) and the cruel
'cures' imposed upon the mentally ill were all in part a consequence of
technical solutions being implemented without reference to the ethical
consequences of their usage. Those who manage such programmes are
rarely cruel, sadistic or indifferent to the needs of their 'victims'; rather,
in order to achieve an end, which they were convinced was attainable
and necessary, they opted to suspend the application of those value criteria that would normally be applied in their relationships with individuals
and groups. Narrowly conceived effectiveness, as a consequence, was
preferred at the expense of humanity. Jordan reminds us that the underlying ethical content of social work decisions is often most evident in

> feelings (often vague, background, niggling feelings) of uneasiness
> and self-reproach, feelings which persist in spite of our forthright
> declarations that we 'had no option' or that 'there was no other
> choice'; in spite of our colleagues' reassurances that we 'can only do
> so much', or that 'in the last resort it is up to people to help them-
> selves'; in spite of our superiors' authoritative pronouncements that
> we were only 'following agency policy', and that to have done other-
> wise would have been to have invited departmental censure. It is the
> mark of a 'burnt-out' social worker that he no longer ever hears, rec-
> ognises or attends to the still small voice of conscience that his less
> cynical and hardened colleagues frequently get inside their heads,
> questioning their good intentions or good faith. It is only by attending
> to such feelings of regret or self-reproach that we can subject our
> work to any sort of active moral scrutiny. (1984, p. 153)

The final and only safeguard for many clients who can have no alternative to the service provided by the social worker is the willingness of the latter to apply strict ethical criteria, and to listen to that 'still small voice' which may offer the clients their only protection against injustice and cruelty. Most clients, unfortunately, are not in a position to act as rational, autonomous consumers. Some can, but they are limited in number, whilst others may be able to do so with regard to some elements of their lives whilst in many respects remaining vulnerable to exploitation and abuse.

Dangers of teamworking

Social workers are educated collectively. As students they are encouraged to work in groups, to share their experiences in seminars and to collaborate with each other. Although they may sit examinations and submit most of their essays for marking on an individual basis, their training and education is infused with notions of collective working. The advantages of collaborative working, of pulling together as a team, are assumed to be self-evidently preferable to any alternative. This ethos continues to have a powerful presence beyond training. Even staff who would cheerfully stab a colleague in the back to secure promotion, or slander those they work with in order to protect themselves from management criticism or disapproval, nevertheless in all public utterances stress the sanctity of the team. With tears in their eyes they can be relied upon to bemoan the absence of team spirit in their offices. Parsloe, in her seminal work on social services teams, stresses that 'getting at the meaning of teams is probably made more difficult by the fact it is a word soaked in positive values. It describes an obviously desirable state of affairs, including co-operation, continuity, a sense of purpose and a means of activating it' (1981, p. 25).

In a more recent study of an area social services office, Pithouse (1987) comments upon the use of the 'happy family' metaphor by workers to describe their team. The language of the 'happy family' is ironically more indicative of reality than its casual usage might imply. As we are aware, family life does not always offer a secure haven: indeed superficial impressions may be, as social workers perhaps more than any other professional group are constantly aware, dangerously misleading. Many family relationships are sustained by deceit and self-denial. Such duplicity also unfortunately characterizes much teamworking. 'Minimal scrutiny – maximum harmony' (Pithouse, 1987, p. 52) is, as Pithouse found, often the end product of placing too high a premium upon the achievement of the elusive perfect team. All too frequently 'team mates negotiate an interactive order that promotes a comfortable harmony and precludes an uncomfortable scrutiny of collegial practice' (Pithouse, 1987, p. 52). The very real danger always exists that individuals will, in order not to weaken the cohesion of the team, refrain not merely from the expression of oppositional views but opt to collude with bad practice. Within the training experience students often encounter staff who replicate the worst examples of such behaviour in the protection from scrutiny of their colleagues (Carter and Jeffs, 1992). Given the centrality of ethical values to the social work task, the need to address the extent of individual responsibility for one's own practice and that of colleagues is required, if only to provide a counterweight to the unquestioning emphasis laid upon sustaining harmonious teams. As Pat White (1989) argues in relation to schools, so also in social work education there may be an urgent need to 'teach courage' and value independence of thought.

Training as panacea

Training is something that looms large within social work. Considerable sums have been spent on in-service training for practitioners. Most social workers assume that their employers have a responsibility to provide opportunities for training and that if legislation, for example, is introduced which impinges upon their work in any substantive way, the employing agency is unquestionably expected to fund training which will both interpret it for them and instruct them on implementation. Control over, and responsibility for, training (and indeed professional post-qualifying education) is something that social workers have surrendered to their employers. This training is often perceived as a benefit and gift, an interpretation continuously enhanced by locating it in expensive settings resplendent with elaborate cuisine. Sadly there is no such thing as a free lunch. The cost that is extracted for this largess is the acquiescence of social workers, a denial of their right to professional autonomy and a reinforcement of employer control. For employers the investment is often productive, creating an intellectual 'dependency culture' amongst social workers which serves to discourage collective attempts seriously to take responsibility for their professional development. Unlike a number of more mature professions, social work has never grasped the crucial need to manage its own professional learning, opting instead to supplant the model of self-education common to most professions (which is inner-directed and controlled by the individual) with the episodic consumption of dollops of employer-endorsed and funded training.

This pattern of employer control over the post-qualifying training sector has now been replicated within the area of initial training. Since the early 1990s employers have exercised pre-eminent control over the content, structure and culture of social work education in Higher and Further Education. Employer-led and competency-based programmes have increasingly become the norm. Whatever the weaknesses of the old courses – and they were in many cases legion – some at least demanded a semblance of independent analysis. For some social workers this experience in their initial training left an affinity for critical thinking regarding their practice. Many will in the future acquire such an approach, but it will have to be developed independently rather than be a natural by-product of their professional education.

Conclusion

The need for the continuous application of critical analysis to practice cannot be over-estimated. It provides both the most effective safeguard for clients and a crucial means by which practice may develop. Individual workers must never over-estimate and neither must they under-estimate the significance of their capacity to influence their environment or control their practice. What all these chapters have shown is that workers, either individually or in unison with colleagues, possess considerable autonomy. This autonomy is always tenuously maintained. Furthermore, it can only be justified if social workers use it positively to protect and enhance the life chances of their clients. Used to gratify their own needs and bolster their status it cannot be either justified or allowed to continue unchecked. Equally, a danger exists that social workers and their managers will exploit areas of discretion to make their own work less taxing at the expense of the client. In this context it is essential that social workers sustain their optimism. There is no better means of achieving this than recognizing the value and need for small victories. All the contributors to this book show that without these it is all too easy to slip into despair and despondency or retreat into overly mechanical approaches to the work. Perhaps this danger has never been greater than it is at present. This moment in the history of social work is an important one, a moment when we must reaffirm a commitment to reflective, ethical, professional practice rather than bureaucratic client management.

Questions to consider

1   Can you learn to be an effective social worker simply by doing the job?
2   On what grounds can it be justified that social workers are more 'managed' than GPs or vicars?
3   What lessons can social workers learn from understanding the history of their profession?
4   How can social workers make sure that they do not simply adopt mechanical modes of practice?
5   Should social workers monitor the behaviour and practice of their colleagues?

References

Abbott, P. and C. Wallace (1990) *The Sociology of the Caring Professions.* Basingstoke: Falmer.
Allan, R. (1990) 'Punishment in the Community' in P. Carter, T. Jeffs and M. K. Smith (eds), *Social Work and Social Welfare Yearbook 2.* Buckingham: Open University Press.
Campbell, B. (1988) *Unofficial Secrets.* London: Virago.
Carlen, P. and J. Wardhaugh (1991) 'Locking up our daughters', in P. Carter, T. Jeffs and M. K. Smith (eds), *Social Work and Social Welfare Yearbook 3.* Buckingham: Open University Press.
Carter, P. and T. Jeffs (1992) 'The hidden curriculum; sexuality in professional education', in P. Carter, T. Jeffs and M. K. Smith (eds), *Changing Social Work and Welfare.* Buckingham: Open University Press.
Cohen, R., J. Coxall, G. Craig and A. Sadiq-Sangster (1992) *Hardship Britain.* London: Child Poverty Action Group.
Craig, G. (1992) 'Managing the Poorest: the Social Fund in Context' in P. Carter, T. Jeffs and M. K. Smith (eds), *Changing Social Work and Welfare.* Buckingham: Open University Press.
Department of Social Security (1992) *Evaluating the Social Fund,* Research Report No. 9. London: HMSO.
Dominelli, L. (1988) *Anti-Racist Social Work.* London: Macmillan.

Franklin, B. (1989) 'Wimps and bullies: press reporting of child abuse', in P. Carter, T. Jeffs and M. Smith (eds), *Social Work and Social Welfare Yearbook 1*. Milton Keynes: Open University Press.

Franklin, B. and N. Parton (eds) (1991) *Social Work, the Media and Public Relations*. London: Routledge.

Griffiths Report (1988) *Community Care: Agenda for Action*. London: HMSO.

Hall, P. (1976) *Reforming the Welfare*. London: Heinemann.

Holdaway, S. and G. Mantle (1992) 'Policy-making in the probation service: a view from the probation committee', in P. Carter, T. Jeffs and M. K. Smith (eds), *Changing Social Work and Welfare*. Buckingham: Open University press.

Home Office (1988) *Punishment, Custody and the Community*, Cmnd 424. London: HMSO.

Jordan, B. (1984) *Invitation to Social Work*. Oxford: Basil Blackwell.

Kelly, D. (1992) 'Following the Leader', *Community Care*, 30 April, pp. 16–17.

King, J. (1991) 'Taking the Strain', *Community Care*, 24 October, pp. 16–17.

Levy, A. and B. Kahan (1991) *The Pindown Experience and the Protection of Children*. Staffordshire County Council.

Llewelyn, S. (1992) 'The Sexual Abuse of Clients by Therapists', unpublished paper, Dept of Psychiatry, University of Edinburgh.

MacLeod, M. and E. Saraga (1988) 'Challenging the Orthodoxy: Towards a Feminist Theory and Practice', *Feminist Review*, 28 (Spring), 16–55.

Marshall, M. (1989) 'The sound of silence: Who cares about the quality of social work with old people?' in C. Rojek, G. Peacock and S. Collins (eds), *The Haunt of Misery*. London: Routledge.

Mann, K. (1992) *The Making of an English 'Underclass'? The Social Divisions of Welfare and Labour*. Buckingham: Open University Press.

Murray, C. (1984) *Losing Ground*. New York: Basic Books.

Oppenheim, C. (1990) *Poverty: The Facts*. London: Child Poverty Action Group.

Parsloe, P. (1981) *Social Services Area Teams*. London: George, Allen & Unwin.

Pithouse, A. (1987) *Social Work: The Social Organisation of an Invisible Trade*. Aldershot: Avebury.

Rees, S. (1978) *Social Work Face to Face*. London: Edward Arnold.

Rutter, P. (1989) *Sex in the Forbidden Zone*. New York: Tarcher.

Schorr, A. (1992) *The Personal Social Services: An Outside View*. York: Joseph Rowntree Foundation.

Seebohm Report (1968) *Report on the Personal and Allied Social Services*. Cmnd 3703. London: HMSO.

Shardlow, S. (ed.) (1989) *The Values of Change in Social Work*. London: Tavistock/Routledge.

Smith, D. (1965) 'Front Line Organization of the State Mental Hospital', *Administrative Science Quarterly*, 10, 381–99.

Smith, G. (1979) *Social Work and the Sociology of Organizations*. London: Routledge & Kegan Paul.

White, P. (1989) 'Educating courageous citizens', in C. Harber and R. Meighan
    (eds), *The Democratic School: Educational Management and the Practice of
    Democracy.* Ticknall: Education Now.
Wilding, G. (1982) *Professional Power and Social Welfare.* London: Routledge
    & Kegan Paul.
Williams, F. (1989) *Social Policy: A Critical Introduction.* Cambridge: Polity
    Press.

Index

182 *Index*